The Flesh Made Word

The Flesh Made Word

FEMALE FIGURES AND WOMEN'S BODIES

HELENA MICHIE

OXFORD UNIVERSITY PRESS
New York   Oxford

OXFORD UNIVERSITY PRESS

Oxford   New York   Toronto
Delhi   Bombay   Calcutta   Madras   Karachi
Petaling Jaya   Singapore   Hong Kong   Tokyo
Nairobi   Dar es Salaam   Cape Town
Melbourne   Auckland

and associated companies in
Berlin   Ibadan

First published in 1987 by Oxford University Press, Inc.,
200 Madison Avenue, New York, New York 10016

First issued as an Oxford University Press paperback, 1989

Oxford is a registered trademark of Oxford University Press

Library of Congress Cataloging-in-Publication Data
Michie, Helena R.
The flesh made word.
Bibliography, p.   Includes index.
1. English literature—19th century—History and criticism.
2. Women in literature.   3. Body, Human, in literature.   4. Women in art.
5. Painting, Victorian.   I. Title.
PR469.W65M5   1987   820'.9'352042   86-5351
ISBN 0-19-504107-0
ISBN 0-19-506081-4 (PBK.)

2 4 6 8 10 9 7 5 3 1
Printed in the United States of America

To my mother,
who chose my first books
and in memory of my father,
who helped me choose my first words.

Acknowledgments

This was written with the support and encouragement of many people. I would especially like to thank Nina Auerbach, whose magic can turn faulty Xerox copies of Pre-Raphaelite paintings into full-color pictures of Victorian women and the moons that haunt them. Thanks also to Elaine Scarry whose work on the body is as inspirational as her support of this project.

I would finally like to acknowledge my enormous debt to Judith Levin and Colleen Lamos whose conversations and comments made this work—and any work—possible.

David DeLaura, Houston Baker, and Ellen Pollak read early versions of the manuscript and commented generously. I am grateful to Oxford University Press for, among other things, assigning this manuscript to a reader as lucid and careful as Margaret Homans.

My heartfelt thanks to Joan Maruyama, Helen Healy, Susan Allen, and William Flesch for their typing, proofreading, and compilation.

It is with great affection that I thank my uncle, Dr. Leopold Wienick for his books and his wisdom in searching out Pre-Raphaelite art, and Scott Derrick for turning days of writing into days of feasting.

February 1986   H.R.M.

Contents

The Flesh Made Word

Introduction:
Constructing the Frame

This book began in many different places. One of these was Rome, Italy, where as a child I would walk down the streets of a city filled with effigies of women. Replicas of the Virgin served as landmarks on my way to kindergarten; a stand down the street sold plastic Marys for 100 lire apiece, while larger Virgins made of stone peered out of niches and alleyways, presided over fountains, stood numbly with plastic flowers at their feet. Bending over the flowers, their babies, and the coins people sometimes threw in their laps, they all wore the same half-secret smiles other people must associate with the Mona Lisa.

On weekends, my parents and I would take trips to museums which were again galleries of women. Several feet above my eye level I could see, ranged on the museum walls, a series of women caught in surprisingly private moments. Looking up, I saw paintings of what seemed to be the same woman bathing, drying her feet, brushing her hair before the mirror. She—the "she" of all paintings, all the baths, and all the mirrors—wore an expression at once proud and secretive as if she both enjoyed the gaze of so many spectators and was embarrassed at her capture at such a moment.

The book began again some five years later on a beach on Long Island, New York, where, stretched out on a lawn chair carefully watching my stomach for signs of sunburn, I first read *Middlemarch*. I could not explain then why I read the description of Dorothea so carefully, or why I asked for sequels, for "more books about Dorothea." I could not begin to answer the more compli-

3

cated question: why the other Victorian novels supplied by my teachers were in some sense "about Dorothea" and why they at least partially satisfied my craving to hear more about her and what she looked like.

In college, as a feminist, I saved Victorian novels, these multiple portraits of Dorothea, for private indulgence, half-ashamed that I could be repeatedly enchanted by texts framed by equally predictable marriages and deaths. Before I graduated, however, I was beginning to understand that I was living and reading a shared obsession, and that Victorian novels had during that period become in some sense the texts of feminism. While I explore some of the possible connections between Victorianism and feminism in the final chapter of this book, I will only say here that continued readings in both the novels of the period and in feminist theory have led me back to the heroine's body as the locus of interpretation, textuality, and the fascination of feminist readers for the novels and for the Dorotheas that give them shape.

By talking about the female body in Victorian fiction and culture, this book continuously inscribes itself at the ever-shifting centers of a series of paradoxes about the Victorian period, about women, and about the project of criticism itself. To look at the intersections of feminism, Victorian studies, and critical theory is to look first at the contradictions within and between these bodies of knowledge.

The Victorian era, once safely ensconced in criticism as the historical site of repression, silence, and prudery, has now been indelibly rewritten by critics and historians of the period as an important period in the transition to the articulation of the sexual. Like Leo Steinberg, who in his *Sexuality of Christ*, looks for the sexual in what has always been assumed to be the place of its erasure, writers as diverse as Michel Foucault, Steven Marcus, Martin Meisel, Peter Gay, and Nina Auerbach have been provoked into producing readings of the Victorian period generated by an awareness of its erotic and linguistic fertility. Foucault explains that prevailing notions of Victorian prudery and silence ignore the period's textualization of sex and its creation of the science of sexology. Gay's "rescue" of Victorian eroticism depends on private discourse, on the letters and journals of Victorian women who struggled to give life and shape to their own erotic experiences. Steven Marcus and

Martin Meisel in *The Other Victorians* and *Realizations*, respectively, look at Victorian sub-genres—pornography and melodrama—to document both the physicality of the world outside the Victorian canon, and the influence of this world on more "canonical" texts of the period, while Nina Auerbach, in *Woman and the Demon*, takes Victorian images of women traditionally associated with sterility, passivity, and victimization to show their underlying mythic and erotic power.[1]

Despite these rescues, Victorianism in both England and America retains enough of its traditional associations to present itself as both contradictory and problematic. As a time of simultaneous obsession with the details of feminine illness and denial of female physicality, of insistence on the measuring and quantifying of bodily secretions and on women's silence about bodily parts as seemingly "innocent" as legs, the Victorian period embodies both the absence and the presence of female sexuality. While the official language of the new Victorian sexology proclaimed women's bodies as the focal point for the analysis of women's roles, women themselves were denied access to the language that generated such verbiage.[2] Although Victorian language—even and perhaps especially women's language—is rich with metaphoric allusions to the body, discussions of the body itself are always immediately supplemented with metaphors from other fields of discourse.

Victorian novels replicate this dis-ease with and within the female body as they replicate the contradiction between its absence and its presence. Although many, even most, Victorian novels center on a physically beautiful heroine and trace the disposition of her body in either marriage or death, the body itself appears only as a series of tropes or rhetorical codes that distance it from the reader in the very act of its depiction. These codes, which are discussed in detail in Chapter IV, have the simultaneous power to frame the heroine and to dissolve themselves to allow for glimpses of her body. Victorian paintings, like the novels, conduct books, and sex manuals of the era, capture and are in turn captured by the interplay between the present and absent female body; Pre-Raphaelite paintings, discussed briefly in Chapter III, for example, announce themselves as highly physical, eroticized portraits of women, only to swathe the body in voluminous clothing, detail, and historical and mythic allusion.

Much recent work on the body, most notably Foucault's and Francis Barker's, has been invaluable in identifying a shift in corporal history, and in tracing the body's entrances into and exits from the historical scene.[3] Both the body and the history that take shape from their arguments, however, seem strangely neuter; the fact of sexual difference even in *The History of Sexuality* is covered over, subsumed under the rubric of class. In *The History of Sexuality Volume I*, for instance, women make only cameo appearances; in the entrance of sex into history they are neither agents nor subjects. In describing the historical transition from sex as behavior to sex as identity, for example, Foucault tells the story of "a farm hand from the village of Lapcourt" who, in 1867, "obtained a few caresses from a little girl, just as he had done before and seen done by the village urchins around him" (*History*, p. 31). Foucault moves from this collapsed biography of the farm hand and the community of men he seems to represent to an interpretation of the incident in light of the "repressive hypothesis":

> What is the significant thing about this story? The pettiness of it all; the fact that this everyday occurrence in the life of village sexuality, these inconsequential bucolic pleasures, could become, from a certain time, the object not only of a collective intolerance but of a judicial action, a medical intervention, a careful clinical examination, and an entire theoretical elaboration.
>
> (*History*, p. 31).

For Foucault, these "inconsequential . . . pleasures," transformed by a particular historical moment into public discourse, would seem to have a potential life outside of discourse, outside significance, outside even of agency or attribution. "These pleasures" belong to no one, except perhaps to the neutral theoretician. The apparent neutrality, the elision of the farm hand and the little girl under the aggregate "bucolic," disguises the fact that the narrative point of view, the subjectivity of the text, is aligned with the chain of men who set up, explain, and interpret the sexual "game of curdled milk," for the little girl and the reader. The spectacular array of texts about the body *as* historical spectacle—again Foucault's and Barker's seem the most compelling—ignores the potentially spectacular fact of sexual difference, the moment when difference becomes visible.

This is, in a sense, why this book is not about men's bodies, although the male body *in* difference, the resexualization of the "neutral" corporeal "he" is a subject that is well worth writing about. The conflation of the body, "woman," and representation might give us a glimpse of the little girl who might or might not enjoy "curdled milk," who might or might not use that name for it, who might or might not see it as an activity that involves her body.

Women, like Victorianism, occupy an uneasy and shifting place at the intersection of the body and its representation. While, as Leonard Barkan notes, the body has, throughout history, been used as a metaphor for apprehending and domesticating the unknown, the normative body of his discourse, like that of Foucault, is indisputably male.[4] Women's bodies occupy no such stable and comforting relation to the unknown; since they are themselves the unknowable, the unpenetrable mystery, they are not so much vehicles of epistemological consolation as they are sources of change, disruption, and complication. This view of the male and female body, of male and female sexuality, persists today; proponents of men's liberation as well as of feminism write directly against a tradition that defines male sexuality as obvious, uncomplicated, and iterable, and female sexuality as mysterious.[5]

Women become both metaphors for the unknowable, and metaphors for metaphor, their bodies figures of figuration. A long philosophical tradition from Locke to Derrida, which I discuss in Chapter IV, links women with metaphor and rhetoric, with language and textuality itself. As Gayatri Spivak puts it: "The discourse of man is in the metaphor of woman." Anthropologists like Claude Levi-Strauss and Gayle Rubin have also identified women as "signs" or "tokens" of culture.[6] An equally long and complex tradition, as Elizabeth Spelman reminds us, identifies woman with the body and the physical, as opposed to language and the intellectual. If women are simultaneously language and body, what does it mean to represent their bodies in language? How can one write across and between these traditions to begin to depict female physicality? Since women's bodies are also simultaneously a primary metaphor for other things (Annette Kolodny has traced, for example, the portrayal of land as a woman's body) and metaphorized into culturally recognized figures at the moment of their depiction (John

Donne and a long series of erotic poets describe women *as* land),
the issues of physical representation become especially complex.[7]
While I do not mean to imply that a "literal" body can be constituted out of language, itself, as Derrida and others have shown,
entirely dependent on metaphor, it is no coincidence that woman
and metaphor should occupy the same ancillary position with re-
gard to "literal" "bodily" truth.[8]

To acknowledge on the one hand the impossibility of full and
literal representation, and on the other to suggest that sexual politics intervene to produce gaps between the representation of the
female body and its "realities," is to implicate oneself in the third
paradox that informs this project, a paradox that can be provi-
sionally labelled theoretical. I will argue that the representation of
the female body is no simple case of *differance*, but a historically
aggravated instance of the violent and marked separation of signifier and signified.

Situated in this series of paradoxes, this book seeks a partial but
not static resolution of them and posits a liberation of the female
body in (but not from) discourse. This liberation is—must be—
muted both rhetorically and politically; I am under no illusion
that women can be freed from patriarchal discourse or rescued
from the political marginality that discourse helps to construe. Instead, I settle for the liberation of movement, again both rhetorically (in the sense of shifting tropes) and politically (in the sense
of "women's movement"). If the tropes that entrap women's
bodies are examined both in their power and in their ability to
dissolve themselves, if women's bodies are seen to appear and to
disappear at particular moments in the text and in history, this
liberation, based on the energy of movement and subversion, will
become a possibility.

The movement between the presence and the absence of the
female body is figured in this book by a continuous series of mirrors. The mirror is itself, of course, simultaneously presence and
absence, depiction, inversion, and distortion of the body. It is also
an image of the body (vanity/surface) and of an attempt to move
beyond the body (reflection/contemplation). This book, then, attempts to construct a funhouse of mirrors that reflect women's
bodies and each other in a self-reproducing series of images: the
prostitute's looking-glass scrawled with clients' names in Dante

Gabriel Rossetti's poem, "Jenny," Hetty Sorrel's mirror in *Adam Bede*, in front of which she creates and destroys herself, Gilbert and Gubar's subversive glass in their reframing and inversion of the tale of Snow White, Lacan's mirror which reflects the self alienated from language, the lesbian mirror in Jane Gallop's *The Daughter's Seduction*, where women turn from reflecting men to reflecting each other, my own "mirror-readings" in Chapter IV where texts are alternately interpreted as affirmations and erasures of the body. This is only a partial list; as mirrors begin to reflect each other, they, in reproducing themselves, begin to produce other mirrors, other images, and other reflections.

One of the main functions of mirrors, both for the heroines I discuss and for the arguments I construct around them, is framing. Like mirrors, frames embody multiple and often contradictory meanings; "frames" can be unjust accusations (hence the once-popular feminist T-shirt "Eve was framed"), ways of keeping women "in their place," protection from a hostile world, or definitions of a space from which women can begin to assert their power. Framing can simultaneously be, as Delores Rosenblum puts it in her article on Christina Rossetti and modeling, a way of being "killed into art," or a way of commanding attention and presenting the body. Betsy Erkkila's reframing of Greta Garbo as a woman who can break outside the framing of male directors, acknowledges the medium of the frame itself as a possible source of power for Garbo and other actresses. Chapters III and IV of this study discuss the various possibilities of heroines framed in language and art as they explore dressing, modeling, and figuration.[9]

While the figures of frame and mirror provide one scaffolding for this study, it is also arranged more broadly around taboos and their dissolution. The first three chapters outline a series of representational taboos that restrict the depiction of women's hunger and work, both of which are associated with the body and with sexuality. Looking at both the empowering and restrictive implications of the connection between food, work, and sex, these chapters focus on the manipulation of these forbidden topics by literary and nonliterary texts and identify textual means of access to them. The fourth chapter is also a study of the interplay between the unrepresentable and its representation; it explores the various codes employed in heroine description, positing synecdoche, cliché, and metaphor as central to both the depiction and erasure of female sexuality. The final chapter locates itself at a historical moment of specular inversion. In it, I move from Victorianism to a discussion of how twentieth-century "second wave" feminists have tried in their writing and in related arts to break through Victorian coding and to reproduce an integrated, totalized female body. In the chapter, I look carefully at a series of feminist poets whose conscious distrust of Victorianism, and of conventional tropes, provides a beginning for a counter poetics. I choose poets rather than novelists—more on this in Chapter V—both because it seems to me that feminist writers, as Margaret Atwood once put it at a reading of her poetry, "work out" issues in poetry first before elaborating on them in prose, and because poetry allows for a condensation of tropes that renders highly visible the rhetorical analysis of Victorianism which, in my view, serves as a basis for so much contemporary feminist writing.

In situating my own response to the responses of feminist poetics to Victorianism I make use of feminist theory, of deconstruction, and of Lacanian psychoanalysis. I attempt, from this triple perspective, to describe both the empowering possibilities of an integrative feminist vision and its limitations as a way of talking about language and representation.

The shift from the nineteenth to the twentieth century, from an emphasis on prose to an emphasis on poetry, disrupts the implied symmetry of this project's engagement with mirrors. Such a disruption is, it seems to me, an appropriate reminder of and a tribute to the distorting and disrupting powers of mirrors themselves. By cutting across illusions of symmetry and closure, and by introducing a series of lives not yet finished and texts not yet made static, Chapter V emphasizes the fluidity of the signifiers "Victorian" and "woman" as they intersect at the point of representation.

The moment that we admit the mirror's failure to reproduce an undistorted image, we are introducing the mirror as material object, the mirror as history. The final chapter is both *about* history in that it outlines a feminist historiography and *is* history in that it describes a particular historical moment. Chapter V, and by extension, this book, locate themselves self-consciously in the flaws in the mirror, in the historic, cognitive, and political barriers to "perfect" reproduction, "perfect" representation.

Because of the grounding of this study in shift and paradox—movements I tentatively identify as "choreographies" in Chapter III—I hesitate throughout, even in close readings, to produce readings that are "closed." My emphasis is not so much on whether a particular depiction of a heroine is "full," "physical," or "sexual" as on the erotic and empowering interplay of sexual possibility with its absence. This means that I pay relatively little attention to whether a particular author is male or female, a work "feminist" or "anti-feminist." Although there is much room for valuable work on the specific historical situation of representation, the focus here is on opening up texts to movement and surprise. I concentrate on reading rather than writing, on language rather than on intention.

By taking many layers of Victorian culture and subculture as its texts, this project necessarily approaches the female body from a series of different angles. While the first two chapters are, broadly speaking, sociohistorical in their emphasis, the third looks more closely at the iconography of the period, the fourth deals mainly with literary theory, and the last with feminist theory and its contributions to the poetics of representation. While the body that emerges from this conflation of approaches may not spring fully realized from my text any more than from the Victorian novels, poems, paintings, and conduct books upon which it is based, I hope that the variety of methodologies will produce for the reader at least an outline of the issues and of a woman's body arrested momentarily in the act of pouring tea, making a speech, flirting, desiring, mothering, writing a novel.

CHAPTER I

Ladylike Anorexia:
Hunger, Sexuality, and Etiquette
in the Nineteenth Century

The dinner table is an important locus of interaction in Victorian culture. In the novel, it is the place where characters, plots, and subplots come together to enjoy and to produce the rich complexities of Victorian fiction. In etiquette and conduct books, it is the central social space where the rules that govern Victorian society are made manifest. Crucial to the dinner party that figures and so prominently figures *in* so many texts of the period is the heroine, whose presence and conversations at these social encounters so profoundly influence their outcome. Conspicuously absent, however, in novels and conduct books that deal so closely with dinners, tea, and other social gatherings is any mention of the heroine eating. Although a Trollope hero can discuss the relative merits of several after-dinner ports for pages, and although we may follow him to his club to watch him eat his daily chop or his soufflé, the Trollope heroine, like her sisters in other texts of the period, laughs, flirts, and presides over presumably empty plates.[1]

Even the Victorian social novel, famous for its realistic treatment of the most harrowing and unpalatable subjects, rarely depicts heroines in the act of either eating or starving. Elizabeth Gaskell mentions at times that Mary Barton is "clemming," but never depicts her hunger with the same detailed accuracy that marks her descriptions of interiors or of children dying. Mary watches her father grow mad and murderous through want of food; she herself grows only a little thinner and paler. Dickens' Little Dorrit floats through the gates of the Marshalsea into the

l world apparently oblivious of her own hunger, refusing to eat
front of anyone at her employer's so she may smuggle food
me to her father. Perhaps as a protest against corporeal bondage,
e refuses food in almost every one of the novel's "prisons,"
iving plate and glass untouched at the Clennam's, Flora's, and
the Marshalsea itself. Hunger in even the poorest Victorian
roines happens offstage; never do they intrude on the decorum
the novel to speak with the frankness of the era's heroines of
onfiction like Mayhew's seamstresses, one of whom reports: "I
ave chewed camphor and drunk water to stay my hunger. My
ains from flatulence have been dreadful."[2]

Despite these gaps in the meticulous realism of the Victorian
ovel, despite the emptiness of the heroine's plate, women's hun-
er constitutes a vital mythic force behind both the novel and the
culture. Gilbert and Gubar and others have discussed Victorian
novels—particularly those by women—as rewritings of the Fall
myth, where women's sexuality, power, and hunger are conflated.[3]
It is in the mythic or metaphoric sub-texts of the novels, then, that
women act out their hunger, reach for and periodically redefine
the apple that is denied to them on realism's apparently seamless
surface, its apparently uncracked plate. Women's hunger operates
with equal force in interstices of Victorian culture; it is as alive in
those generic "sub-texts" of the period—etiquette books, beauty
and sex manuals, pornography—as it is in the sub-texts of canonical
novels. As hunger, which figures unspeakable desires for sexuality
and power, becomes itself silenced by Victorian euphemism, a
metonymic chain is set in motion where hunger is displaced from
the "center" of literature and culture, first onto metaphor, and
then onto sub-literary genres.

This chapter focuses first on sub-genre, then on sub-text by identifying the structuring power of the Fall myth and the place it
allows for the expression of female "appetite" in conduct books,
sex manuals, and in canonical and noncanonical novels of the
period. Jane Eyre's temptation to commit bigamy in Rochester's
apple orchards, Alec D'Urberville's forcing of the strawberry into
Tess' reluctant and puzzled lips, and the Countess _____'s warning in her conduct book, *Good Society* that "the onion is the forbidden fruit of the modern Eve,"[4] all simultaneously admonish
women to keep their mouths firmly shut, and emphasize the prob-

INDIGESTION DELICATELY DESCRIBED.

Mamma. "WHERE IS YOUR PAIN, MY DARLING?"

Edith. "O—JUST IN THAT PLACE WHERE A DOLL'S WAX ENDS; AND IT GOES ALL THE WAY DOWN TO MY LEGS!"

From *Punch*, Oct. 7, 1871, photograph by Allan Kobernick.

lem of female hunger. While, as this chapter will explain, Tess, Jane, and the polite young lady celebrated in conduct books are never actually seen eating, the issue of their relation to food and to the desires it comes to represent is central to the understanding of Victorian sexual politics and to the problem of representation itself.

Sex manuals consistently equate food, especially certain types of food, and lust. In Beckland's *Physiological Mysteries and Revelations of Love*, the author claims that excessive appetites of all kinds lead directly to sexual malfunction: "eating hard salt things and spices, the body becomes more and more heated, whereby the desire for venereal embraces is very great."[5] He urges a light vegetable diet that simultaneously "cools ardor" and "produces children." Impotence can be cured by eating appropriate foods; his litany of aphrodisiacs is both long and specific: "syrup of pine apples . . . port wine . . . mushrooms roasted and steeped in salad oil . . . artichokes, figs, potatoes, shell-fish, peaches, eggs, oysters" (Beckland, p. 28). He goes on to explain that meagre meals are a "corrective of puberty" and that people with the strongest sex drives eat the richest and spiciest foods. As late as 1905, manuals connected masturbation in girls with "desiring mustard, pepper, vinegar and spices . . . which appetites are certainly not natural for little girls."[6]

Not surprisingly, according to the logic that links hunger, spice, richness, and sex, foods themselves are assigned a gender. The most feminine food—or meal—of all is tea, where as M. E. Braddon puts it, in *Lady Audley's Secret*, at "the tea table women are most fairy-like, most feminine."[7] Rich, meaty, or very spicy foods, on the other hand, are identified as "male." Gilbert and Gubar cite the example of the heroine in *Castle Rackrent* who is forced in a metaphorical rape scene to eat pork, sausages, and other food from pigs.[8] In E. D. E. N. Southworth's *Self-Raised or From the Depths*, the heroine's villainous and titled husband takes her to England, where, instead of introducing her to the highest circles of society, he hides her in squalid hotels. The most vivid image of her torture is not her husband's contemptuous cruelty, but the fact that the hotel smells of "meat, onions and tobacco smoke,"[9] foods and odors to which the heroine has apparently never been exposed. Claudia is further repulsed and insulted when her husband proceeds to eat in front of her. Lord Vincent "falls" on his beef and ale, "the fumes of which soon filled the room" (Southworth, p. 149). But the worst is yet to come, as Claudia is exposed to the malest of pastimes and the malest of scents: her husband proceeds to light a pipe and to fill the room with tobacco smoke. When asked whether she does not like the smell, Claudia replies that she does not know since no gentleman has ever smoked in front of her before. The unmistakable phallic nature of cigars and pipes serves as an equally unmistakable sign of male dominance and betrayal; when Jane Eyre encounters Rochester under the apple trees in the first "false" proposal scene she detects his presence by the smell of his cigar.

Delicate appetites are linked not only with femininity, but with virginity. In the century's most influential and most reprinted sex manual, *Aristotle's Master-Piece*, the author describes "green-sickness," a disease common to virgins which manifests itself in a "loathing of meat" and of "raw or burnt flesh."[10] Although he clearly regards this condition as a disease which must be cured in order for women to embrace marriage successfully, he makes it equally obvious that the illness can be used as a test of virginity. The typical period of illness undergone by many fictional Victorian heroines just before they admit love for a particular man, an illness often seen as an expression of fear of sexuality and of assertion of manipulative control, can also be seen then in the light of such a proof. Weakness, pallor, and rejection of food are signs of transition in the refined heroine, as for the first time she contemplates marriage and related sexual "duties."[11]

The use of inflated Fall rhetoric as a warning to women against eating too much or eating the wrong kind of food reveals an uneasiness with women's hunger that reaches far beyond the dinner table. Countess _____'s strictures against the onion were nominally inspired by the onion's smell—she did not want young ladies to have bad breath. Clearly, however, there is something more fundamental at work; in another manual we learn that the onion is "the root of Aphrodite."[12] Etiquette books rushed to present dinner as a time to gather one's moral forces:

> Every luxurious table is a scene of temptation, which it requires fixed principles and an enlightened mind to withstand. . . . Noth-

ing can be more seducing to the appetite than this arrangement
of the viands which compose a feast; as the stomach is filled, and
the natural desire for food subsides, the palate is tickled by more
delicate and relishing dishes until it is betrayed into excess.[13]

An 1896 attack on strictures against women's eating begins with
the equation of starvation and feminine spirituality. In *The Diary
of a Greedy Woman*, the author parodies the transformation of
religious belief into a social grace:

> If the vineyard yielded wine and the orchard fruit . . . they
> [men in the Dark Ages] believed it was that men might forswear
> the delight thus offered. . . . [T]his lingered among woman . . .
> Christian duty became a new feminine grace   (Pennell, p. 10).

She continues in the idiom of deflation:

> . . . and where the fanatic has fasted that his soul might prove
> comelier in the sight of God, silly matrons and maidens starved,
> or pretended to starve themselves, that their bodies might seem
> fairer in the eyes of men   (Pennell, p. 10).

In what is essentially a cookbook, Pennell humorously and cate-
gorically explodes the central myths of Victorian femininity. She
insists that eating a lot makes one look younger ("gluttony is the
best cosmetic"), and that "woman is *lovely* in the act of eating"
(Pennell, p. 11). She even goes so far as to turn the association
of hungry women and coarseness on its head by claiming that
woman is "made of coarser clay than man" because she does not
enjoy food properly. The language of this defense of women's
hunger, this need to invert cultural myths, suggests the lengths to
which nineteenth-century culture was willing to go to deny
women's physical need for food.

The portrait of the appropriately sexed woman, then, emerges
as one who eats little and delicately. She is as sickened by meat as
by sexual desire. Pregnant women, even more than virgins, are
supposed to have no appetite unless the child is a boy, in which
case a healthy woman "longs for food" (Aristotle, p. 45), as, presumably, the fetus inside her begins to show signs of appropriate
masculine hunger.

The vision of the delicate young lady has, of course, a class as
well as a gender component. A lady does not need to eat both be-

cause she does not have male "desires" and because she does little
to work up an appetite of any sort. Her femininity and her social
position are defined quite literally by negation; denial of hunger
is an affirmation of a precarious class position. In *Eve's Daughters:
Common Sense For Maid, Wife, and Mother*, Marian Harland
ridicules the typical "young miss" of the time:

> It is a circumstance at once fortunate and notable, if she does not
> take the notion into her pulpy brain that a healthy appetite for
> good, substantial food is "not a bit nice," "quite too awfully vul-
> gar, you know." She would be disgraced in her own opinion and
> lose caste with her refined mates were she to "eat like a plow-
> boy."[14]

The rhetoric of class is quite obvious here; the young lady's fear
of "losing caste" becomes, additionally, a sexual matter with the
image of the plowboy.

If food is both a moral and a class question, dining rituals take
on the serious purpose of defining moral good and upholding class
structure. The language of etiquette books leaps from notions of
what is polite to pronouncements on what is moral. It is not surprising that the Fall and its network of related images appear in
defense of something so apparently trivial as the eating or non-
eating of onions. The Countess _____ remarks:

> How to eat soup and what to do with a cherry-stone are weighty
> considerations . . . taken as the index of social status; and it is
> not too much to say that a young woman who elected to take
> claret with her fish or eat peas with her knife would justly risk the
> punishment of being banished from good society
> (Countess, p. 170).

The words "justly" and "good" in this passage move beyond con-
siderations of social class into the more complicated arena of morality. A lapse in table manners becomes a fall from grace, and the
spectre of the fallen woman banished from society rises up before
the dinner table at the Countess' sanctimonious conclusion.

The complicated, coded behaviors required of the polite young
lady extend to all areas of dining. One major focus of debate in
the etiquette books is the delicate way to eat cherries: "Very
dainty feeders press out the stone with a fork in the first in-

stance. . . . This is the safest way for ladies" (Countess, p. 170). Again, the word "safe" has moral connotations; lapses from etiquette become dangerous to the reputations of the young women involved. It is probably not a coincidence that most of the examples of "unsafe" behavior which lead to this domesticated version of the Fall revolve around fruit; one advice manual warns men, "Don't touch fruit with [your] fingers when preparing it for a lady" (Countess, p. 170), as if the offering of fruit with the hands is too close a reenactment of the moment of temptation in the garden.

The Fall is itself so sensitive a topic that both etiquette books and works of fiction hesitate in actually naming it. In his preface to *The Vicar of Bullhampton*, Trollope feels he has to justify depicting a fallen woman to an audience of young lady readers, while in her preface to the second edition of *Ruth*, Gaskell goes so far as to apologize for treating the matter at all. In Dina Mulock Craik's *A Woman's Thoughts About Women*, the author goes through the same process of hesitation before concluding that the subject must be addressed.[15] The silence that surrounds the depiction of the fallen woman allows the Fall to be used as a metaphor for other things; its monitory power converges on seemingly minor—even innocent—issues of daily life. The spectre of the fallen woman comes in from the streets to haunt the dining room of the middle-class home.

It is only a small step from stringent moralistic rules about dining to a complete condemnation of a lady's eating. Lewis Carroll was reportedly fearful that the little girls with whom he loved to surround himself would eat too much, and it seems that he equated eating with other "sins of the flesh."[16] One etiquette manual describes the process of secret or binge eating which we would now refer to as bulimia, an important corollary of anorexia nervosa:

> It is not that they [young women] absolutely starve themselves to death, for many of the most abstemious at the open dinner are the most voracious at the secret luncheon. Thus the fastidious dame whose gorge rises before company at the sight of a single pea, will on the sly swallow cream tarts by the dozen, and caramels and chocolate drops by the pound's weight.[17]

The same book bemoans the equation of eating with coarseness in young women:

> Many of our over-refined dames seem to have adopted Lord Byron's notion, that eating is unbecoming to woman. It is a marvel that some of them manage to keep body and soul together with the apparent regimen of starvation to which they subject themselves   (*Bazar*, p. 193).

Weakness and pallor became signs of beauty in the "over-refined." This aesthetics of deprivation forced eating to become a private activity and abstemiousness a public avowal of femininity: "A delicate appetite was much preferred, and young women might be forced to nibble scraps in their bedroom so they might face the dinner table with ladylike anorexia."[18] The "secret nibbling in the bedroom" makes even more explicit the unconscious equation of food and sex. Eating is typed as a bedroom activity, something too personal to survive the public scrutiny of the dinner table. The shame associated with eating is also, interestingly enough, typical of the modern anorectic who will hide food in her own room and perform elaborate rituals to disguise the fact that she is eating.[19]

This movement into the privacy of the bedroom is reenacted in the fiction of the period. The narrator of Elizabeth Gaskell's *Cranford* describes Miss Jenkyns' customary way of eating oranges:

> When oranges came in, a curious proceeding was gone through. Miss Jenkyns did not like to cut the fruit; for, as she observed, the juice all ran out nobody knew where; sucking (only I think she used some more recondite word) was in fact the only way of enjoying oranges; but then there was the unpleasant association with a ceremony frequently gone through by little babies; and so, after dessert, in orange season, Miss Jenkyns and Miss Matty used to rise up, possess themselves each of an orange in silence, and withdraw to the privacy of their own rooms, to indulge in sucking oranges.[20]

The seriousness with which Miss Jenkyns ponders the problem of how to eat the fruit, taken in conjunction with the retreat to the bedroom, betrays the codedness of the orange and its central place in the values of class and sex that serve as foundations for the town of Cranford.

The fall into hunger, like women's initial fall from grace, is recuperable only by the figure of the Virgin Mary. Mary comes to stand not only for chastity but for fasting as well:

> Fasting, like chastity, was prescribed for both sexes, but like virginity, fasting has a particular goal in women that enhances the symbolism of wholeness and purity. Amenorrhea, the absence of menstruation, develops rapidly. Even young girls on a minor diet can miss a period, while starvation (as in the case of the illness anorexia nervosa) can cause permanent damage; menstruation might never begin again.[21]

Fasting, then, purifies the body by obliterating signs of sexuality; the Virgin Mary, predictably, inverts the fall by replacing sexuality with chastity, hunger with self-denial.

"Ladylike anorexia" became inscribed and prescriptive as fashion began to decree smaller and smaller waists. Ehrenreich, English, and others from the nineteenth and twentieth centuries have detailed the physical dangers women underwent in trying to squeeze their bodies into corsets; according to *For Her Own Good*, corsets sometimes put so much pressure on internal organs that the uterus was squeezed out through the vagina.[22] The more protectionist of Victorian etiquette books and the majority of feminist pamphlets spoke out against the abuses of tight lacing, but their vehemence only attests to how ingrained the notion of daintiness and small-waistedness was in Victorian culture. Young women and fictional heroines alike tried to change their body shape to fit their clothes, which in turn assume the shape of normative femininity. Rose, the heroine of Alcott's *Eight Cousins*, will not loosen a favorite belt for fear that her waist will grow bigger and she will no longer be able to wear it.[23]

There is a close relationship between the ideal Victorian young lady, as she is construed and constructed by etiquette books, and her fictional counterpart, the heroine. The figure of the delicate heroine passes repeatedly from fiction to reality and back again. Thinness and "interesting pallor," for example, became the defining characteristic of the early Victorian heroine as well as the lady of the period. In his parodic novel, *The Heroine*, E. S. Barrett has Cherry mourn her good health and appetite as rendering her unfit for the role of heroine she so badly wants to play: " 'What a name—Cherry! It reminds one so much of plumpness and a ruddy health. Cherry—better be called Pineapple at once. There is a grey and yellow melancholy in Pineapple that is infinitely preferable.' "[24] The pun on "pine-apple" aligns Cherry with a modern-day version of Eve, whose heroinism is defined by resistance to her own "pining." Once again the fruit metaphor surfaces, and once more it is tied in with a preoccupation with daintiness and femininity expressed by ill health.

Even though some Victorian works on beauty espouse "plumpness" in young women, the most positive female characters in nineteenth-century novels are most often frail and weak. Elizabeth Gaskell, the Brontes, and even George Eliot use plumpness in their female characters as a sign of a fallen nature. In *Villette*, Ginevra Fanshawe grows visibly fatter as she draws closer to her elopement; in fact, she often eats the "lion's share" of Lucy's bread, cream, and wine, while Lucy, silent, sanctimonious, and puritanical, refuses food throughout the novel. Hetty Sorrel is also characterized by her plumpness and by her associations with cream and other dairy products, while Dinah grows thin sharing her bread with the poor.

The same culture that produced a manual with a chapter entitled "Plumpness: How to Acquire It"[25] used as its models of morality heroines who were physically small and weak. The tiny and even "insignificant" Lucys and Fannys win out over their statuesque and more sophisticated rivals in almost every Trollope novel; bigger, more strikingly beautiful women are somehow suspect.[26] The paradoxical demands of nineteenth-century culture are seen most clearly in the ideal of the hourglass figure which, in effect, prescribes that women live in two bodies at the same time: they must have the breasts and hips of a sensuous woman and the waistline of a schoolgirl. The same culture that advocated padding the bust, shoulders, and back demanded that women wear corsets (Walker, p. 168).

The aesthetic of weakness and hunger only thinly disguises an ideology of male dominance. In an attempt perhaps to invert the original story of the Fall, Victorian novels, popular and canonical, are filled with examples of men taking in starving young women, feeding them, and eventually marrying them. The whole class of "governess novels," so popular with the Brontes and other less well-known writers, is based on the motif of the male employer providing food and shelter. Jane Eyre makes much of her debt to Edward Rochester in a novel obsessed with feeding and starvation. In a short story from *Godey's Lady's Book* entitled "My Wife and Where I Found Her," the narrator who has "lost all faith in women" of his class spots his future wife under an apple tree, washing clothes. What attracts him to her, besides the image of a woman degrading herself before a traditional image of female power and rebellion, is that she pauses every now and then in her work to press her hand to her side as if she is too frail to go on.[27] Predictably, the narrator discovers the young woman is hungry and poor, and provides her with his washing to do. Once her immediate physical wants are satisfied, he applies himself to appeasing her hunger for knowledge and becomes her tutor. It is only a short step from this to marriage. The short story encapsulates a journey from physical to mental to emotional dependency that is set off by a woman's physical hunger. The delicate woman who does not assert her physical needs serves to recuperate the Fall and to reestablish lost innocence. Mythologically, her role is to refuse the apple and to keep her mouth firmly shut to temptation.

The issue of hunger in canonical Victorian literature might at first seem to be summed up in Oliver Twist's frightened cry for "more." The very articulation, however, of his physical needs sets Oliver apart from female characters like Jane Eyre who chokes down her burnt porridge in silence. While Oliver can at least assert his desire, his very physical presence, to the hierarchy of his orphanage, Jane has to sneak to Miss Temple's room for toast and seed cake. Female hunger cannot be acted out in public; once again, it is relegated to bedrooms and closets.

Women's hunger and the attempt to appease it occupy an important place in the Victorian canon. Heroines can have their hunger turned against them or turn their hunger into energy to fight for what they want. Hunger is both dangerous and potentially liberating; it can lead to fulfillment or obsession.

In *Tess of the D'Urbervilles* and *Jane Eyre*, the male protagonists, who run the gamut from villain to romantic hero, all use the heroine's hunger as a means of control. Perhaps the most vivid use of the eating motif is the symbolic rape through food. When Alec forces strawberries on Tess he is not only foreshadowing his rape of her, but also Angel's silencing the story of her life. Forced between Tess' lips, the strawberry silences her protests and effectively prevents her from expressing her own desire from then on. Angel's reaction to Tess is merely the mirror image of Alec's; instead of forcing his sexuality on her, he insists on denying hers. At one point in the novel, he teases her about tasting like milk, bread, and honey, the pure foods on which she principally lives. Like Alec's strawberries, the milk represents a forced feeding of an image onto Tess' personality; red and white images conflate to become the symbolic backbone of the novel, but both are inaccurate, both exaggerations of Tess as she is and as she sees herself.

In the first half of *Jane Eyre*, Rochester, like Alec, uses food and food imagery to control Jane. From the first meeting in Hay Lane, Rochester insists to Jane that she is an elf, a goblin, a fairy, ethereal. When she explains that she was schooled at Lowood, a place where she was almost starved, he exclaims, "No wonder you have rather the look of another world."[28] In his eyes, Jane does not need physical sustenance; her "otherworldliness" is his expression of her lack of physical presence. When he repeatedly observes that he feels she is part of his "own flesh," the romantic rhetoric of his speech disguises the sinister implication that she has no flesh of her own.

Jane's ethereality stands, for Rochester, in complete contrast to Blanche's fleshliness. While he is feasting with Blanche and his other guests, Jane is forced to forage with Adele for food: "everybody downstairs was too engaged to think of [them]" (*Jane Eyre*, p. 201). In the end it is Adele who perceives Rochester's dangerous misconception of Jane. When, once again romantically, he tells Adele he is taking Jane away to the moon, the child anxiously responds that he will starve her—there is no food on the moon.

Jane's return to Rochester and her rejection of St. John's pragmatic proposal of marriage have often been seen as her acceptance of her own physical desires. The process of acknowledging physical needs, however, begins before she meets St. John when, starving, she goes begging from door to door. Her admission "I was a human being and had a human being's wants" is a declaration of her own hunger in the face of Rochester's rhetoric (*Jane Eyre*, p. 396). The rest of the novel translates the literal hunger she feels in her wanderings into a hunger for passionate love. The intermediate step, acknowledging that she needs *food*, is a crucial one in her loving struggle with Rochester and with a world that commands her to efface herself and her needs.

Even in the most loving relationships, food and drink can be used as instruments of minor torture. In *Villette*, Dr. John taunts Paulina with ale; he holds the cup over her head and claims the drink is "deliciously sweet." When he finally allows her to have a sip she discovers, like the model of femininity that she is, that it is far too bitter for her taste.

In response, perhaps, to the dangerous possibilities of expressing hunger, some Victorian heroines use its opposite, physical self-denial, to manipulate their lovers and families. Carroll Smith-Rosenberg has pointed out that illness, for many Victorian women, was a last gasp for power, an effort to maintain control over their single, shrinking resource: their bodies.[29]

Madeline Stavely in Trollope's *Orley Farm* suffers from an ambiguously fictitious lack of appetite when she all but goes on a hunger strike because her mother thinks her lover, Felix, is unsuitable. Her mother notices with horror Madeline's refusal to eat meat, and is quickly convinced that Felix should be accepted into the family. The very speed with which the syndrome is recognized and capitulated to is symptomatic of the codedness of Madeline's behavior.[30] Many other Victorian heroines also fall mysteriously ill at the critical moment between their admission of love and the hero's proposal. The first sign of such an illness—usually the refusal to eat—is a symptom of a predictable malady that will end either in marriage or death. Interestingly, the disease begins when most doctors agree anorexia nervosa occurs: at the moment when the heroine realizes her own sexuality (Bruch, p. xii). The Victorian heroine, like the anorectic, is punishing both her body for its desires and her parents and friends for not recognizing them.

Madeline and her delicate sisters, like Molly in *Wives and Daughters*, and Caroline in *Shirley*, threaten their lovers, families, and readers with their own disappearance from the texts they so cautiously inhabit; they will grow smaller, frailer, and more transparent in search of a happy ending. Trollope goes so far as to turn the masochistic/manipulative hunger metaphor around by claiming that women *feed* sorrow and men starve it; the paradox of feeding starvation is the source of power for these otherwise powerless young women.

The limited power of "feeding," in all senses, is accorded to women. Victorian heroines prepare and serve food for Victorian heroes; it may pass through women's hands but they must not taste it. Shirley Keeldar reminds Caroline in *Shirley* that "choice wines and foods are of no importance" to young women—they are for the gentlemen.[31] In *Villette*, little Polly begs for the best breads, jams, and jellies for Graham, but will not touch them in case anyone suspects her of asking for them on her own account.

Victorian novels also reflect the class component of the formula equating delicate appetites and ladyhood. In *Cranford*, the ladies who form the town's select first circle are reduced by poverty to serving only the lightest refreshments at their card parties. They make a virtue out of their poverty, however, by translating it into transcendent class terms:

> . . . it was considered "vulgar" (a tremendous word in Cranford) to give anything expensive, in the way of eatable or drinkable, at the evening entertainments. Wafer bread-and-butter and sponge biscuits were all that the Honourable Mrs. Jamieson gave; and she was sister-in-law to the late Earl of Glenmire, although she did practise such "elegant economy"   (Cranford, p. 42).

Mrs. Gibson, the benignly contemptible stepmother in Gaskell's *Wives and Daughters*, thrives on the appearance of abstemiousness. From the beginning of her marriage to Dr. Gibson, she tries to redeem the household's vulgar tastes in food, first by not allowing Molly and her father to eat their favorite bread and cheese (it is only "fit for the kitchen"), and then by redesigning the house so that "hot savory-smelling dishes from the kitchen" do not penetrate into the parlor to offend the sensibilities of "highborn ladies with noses of aristocratic refinement."[32] She also tries to impress luncheon guests with the fact that she is too delicate to eat meat during the day and tries to convince Dr. Gibson's medical colleagues of both her superior class position and her feminine ill health by only picking at her food in front of them.

Metaphors of food and hunger—always, of course, related to the larger metaphor of the Fall—can be used to produce a moral taxonomy of female characters. Lucy Snowe's description of the painting of the fallen Cleopatra is important here; Lucy literally equates fleshliness (fatness) with promiscuity:

> It represented a woman, considerably larger, I thought, than the life. I calculated that this lady, put into a scale of magnitude suitable for the reception of a commodity of bulk, would infallibly turn from fourteen to sixteen stone. She was, indeed, extremely well fed; very much butcher's meat—to say nothing of bread, vegetables and liquids—must she have consumed to attain that breadth and height, that wealth of muscle, that affluence of flesh.[33]

The process of identification is harder if a woman's physical appearance does not fit in with the mythology of fallen womanhood. Hetty Sorrel associates herself with what I have called images of pure and virtuous womanhood: butter, cream, and other dairy products. Hetty does such a good job of portraying the innocent maiden that no one notes her "fleshliness," although she is eight months pregnant. Hetty's body, although in one sense the focus of the novel, is unnoticed by her relatives *or* her lover.

In an immediate sense, George Eliot's heroines literally stand out from the crowd of tiny women who serve as the moral focus for so many Victorian novels. Their bigness attests to an inner rebellion against normative femininity; Maggie casts her own difference from canonical heroines in strictly physical terms, for example, when she contrasts herself with her blond, dainty cousin Lucy. Both Maggie and Dorothea Brooke, the most majestic of Eliot's heroines, however, are cut down to size by forces far larger and more powerful than they; patriarchy, destiny, and the conventions of the Victorian novel all converge to reshape them and to rechannel their bigness. Maggie loses her physical power in the water that first destroys her reputation and then kills her, while Dorothea, also the victim of water, "spends" her "full nature . . . in channels which had no great name on earth."[34]

Fallen women can also disguise themselves as little girls. Alice in Wonderland's fall through the rabbit hole propels her into an orgy of eating and drinking. Eating, even little girls' eating, is identified with the Fall in the following dialogue with a pigeon:

"You're a serpent; and there's no use denying it. I suppose you'll be telling me next that you never tasted an egg!"

"I have tasted eggs, certainly," said Alice, who was a very truthful child; "but little girls eat eggs quite as much as serpents do, you know."

"I don't believe it," said the Pigeon; "but if they do, why, then they're a kind of serpent: that's all I can say."

This was such a new idea to Alice, that she was quite silent for a minute or two. . . .[35]

Nina Auerbach explains: "The eggs suggest the woman she will become, the unconscious cannibalism involved in the very fact of eating and desire to eat, and finally, the charmed circle of childhood itself."[36] The association of eggs, the symbol of womanhood, with the serpent evokes more than cannibalism; it harks back to the first destruction of life by eating in the Garden of Eden. Eating, in *Alice*, then, is not merely sexual, but fatal. The "charmed circle of childhood" is the circle of a woman's life; it is both womb and tomb.

If Eve's desire for the apple represents the decentering force of women's power, it is also deeply linked with the question of authority and, finally, of authorship. By eating the apple and precipitating herself and Adam into a newly imagined world upon which she must place her own stamp, Eve is truly "author" of the Fall and of the world in which humankind is forced to live. Adam, who in Eden is referred to as Eve's "author and disposer," is powerless to author or dispose after Eve's initial decision, her truly "original" sin. Women's hunger, associated not only with the orality of eroticism or eating, is also linked, in the novel, to speech and to writing. The figure of *Little Women*'s Jo March stuffing apples into her mouth as she writes in her garret becomes a central one in the feminist recuperation of the "authority" taken up by women in the act of falling. The Victorian women authors who obsessively rewrote the Fall myth[37] were simultaneously transgressing in their hunger to write and to know, and translating trespass into the source of their power.

The anorexia at the center of many Victorian texts turns the act of reading into a diagnosis, the text itself into a symptomology. The novel in particular confronts us with a variety of "symptoms," those gaps in realism that are themselves signs of dis-ease. Paradoxically, then, the seemingly bodiless text turns before our eyes into the semblance of a Victorian woman's body to be constantly, almost obsessively, watched and charted in much the same way that "real" female bodies were treated by Victorian physicians. The body and sexuality assert themselves, like Esther Summerson's in *Bleak House*, through pain and scarring. In learning to read the scars we read desire.

CHAPTER II

Becoming Public Women: Women and Work

The paradox that characterizes nineteenth-century representations of women's hunger—its banishment to the margins as a taboo and its rich and compelling return in the metaphoric subtexts of Victorian culture—is replicated in the representation of women's work. Because, like eating, women's work was perceived as closely involving women's bodies, it is rarely represented in canonical texts; banning work and eating becomes a way of banning or censoring the female body. The dense metaphoric networks associated with women's work, however, make the representations of it that do exist all the more compelling, physical and sexual. The language that describes women's work—sparse as it is in the Victorian canon—focusses the attention of the reader on the apparently marginalized female body by its rich and varied use of physical metaphor.

By the middle of the nineteenth century, physicians had constructed two entirely different bodies for working-class and leisure-class women. Despite the unhealthy and often dangerous working conditions, poor housing and sanitation, and extremely limited access to health care available to the average working-class woman, as Barbara Ehrenreich and Dierdre English point out:

> The medical profession as a whole . . . maintained that it was affluent women who were most delicate and most in need of medical attention. "Civilization" had made the middle-class woman sickly; her physical frailty went hand-in-white-gloved-hand with her modesty, refinement and sensitivity. Working class women were robust, just as they were supposedly "coarse" and immodest.[1]

Between these two ideological/anatomical constructions, the delicate upper-class woman who had to be protected from and nursed through the "sexual storms" of menstruation, pregnancy, and menopause, and the factory worker who was not permitted to take time off for childbirth, lay the chasm of work outside the home (Ehrenreich, pp. 110, 113). Given the physical nature of Victorian perceptions of the differences between working-class and leisure-class women, it is not surprising that such work was seen and discussed in terms of metaphors of the body; women's work, along with eating, took place in the complex Aesopian network of language that simultaneously revealed and erased women's bodily experience.

Women who earned their bread, or in Trollope's more extended metaphor, their "bread and cheese,"[2] inevitably made their bodies, as well as their work, public. The angel who left her house was, on some metaphorical level, seen by the more conservative elements of Victorian culture as a streetwalker. The connection between worker and whore is less surprising in Victorian discussions of working-class women who did, in fact, frequently turn to prostitution to supplement or replace impossibly low wages, but it surfaces less predictably and more subtly in assessments of any kind of paid work for women.

Factories in particular were seen as "temptations" for women to abandon their homes and children, while providing an atmosphere that bred licentiousness. Wanda Fraiken Neff summarizes the conditions that were supposed to "lead to moral degradation":

> The coarse surroundings of the young girl in the factory, the prevalence of indecent language, the absence of dressing-rooms, the necessity of working in scanty clothing because of the heat, the precocious sexual development which was believed to result from heat and confinement, the long hours and the night work which made it necessary to be out on the streets alone, the exhaustion which led to thirst, and the monotonous labor which brought a craving for excitement, were all studied carefully in relation to their effect upon morals.[3]

Predictably, the various "appetites" whetted by factory work were figured in fiction by a description of the coarse and inappropriate foods craved and eaten by factory workers. In *The Wrongs of Women* by Charlotte Tonna, Ann, a young milliner's apprentice,

From *Punch*, July 4, 1863, photograph by Allan Kobernick.

compares the "coarse bread" and "rancid butter" provided for her by her employer to the "light bread and delicate cream" she has left behind in her country home. In Gaskell's "Libby Marsh's Three Eras," the spinners lose "all natural, healthy appetite for simple food" after having worked in the factory all day and, "having no higher tastes, [find] their greatest enjoyment in their luxurious meals." These, to Libby's amazement, consist of "ham, hot bread, eggs and cream" (Neff, p. 49).

It is not only the factories, however, that tempt women away from strict chastity. In Trollope's *The Way We Live Now*, middle-aged Lady Carbury's attempts to earn money by writing *necessarily* remove her from the moral purity of her daughter and other leisure-class Trollope heroines. In an attempt to obtain a positive review of her book she allows an influential editor to kiss her. The narrator ironically dismisses the incident:

> Of course when struggles have to be made and hard work done, there will be little accidents. The lady who uses a street cab must encounter mud and dirt which her richer neighbor, who has a private carriage, will escape. She would have preferred not to be kissed; but what did it matter (*The Way We Live Now*, p. 12).

The use of "street," "dirt," and "little accidents" metaphorically suggest the streetwalker; the kiss extends the suggestion metonymically. By dismissing the incident with an ironic, "but what did it matter," Trollope draws a rigid line between Lady Carbury and his numerous leisure-class heroines like Lucy Roberts or Grace Crawley, who spend a great deal of time and many pages worrying about the propriety of having kissed even the men they love and to whom they are soon to be engaged.

The conservative position that aligned work outside the home with prostitution was only one Victorian tendency. Two other competing schools, which I will call, for convenience's sake, protectionist and protofeminist, deny or modify this connection between work and eroticism but still articulate their position in the language of the body. While conservatives focussed on sexual fall, protectionists focussed on disease, and the protofeminists, paradoxically enough, on the healthy effects of work and the moral and physical corruption that attended idleness.

All three schools expressed themselves in the same idiom; using women's bodies as their rhetorical source, they appropriated images of disease, physical decay, and improper sexuality for their own purposes. Trollope's connection between work and prostitution is inverted in Florence Nightingale's contention that idleness leads to erotic daydreams[4] and in Dinah Mulock Craik's conviction that lack of occupation leads to delusions of love:

> "Many think they are in love when in fact they are only idle" is one of the truest sayings of that great wise bore, Imlac in *Rasselas*, and it has been proved by many a shipwrecked life, of girls especially. This "falling in love" being usually a delusion of fancy, and not the real thing at all, the object is usually unattainable or unworthy.[5]

Protectionist Charlotte Tonna's decaying and consumptive female workers contrast sharply with Anna Jameson's healthy, happy nurses, who are transformed by their work into beauties. Jameson quotes Tennyson's "The Princess" to make her point:

> The maidens came, they talked,
> They sang, they read, till she, not fair,
> began
> To gather light,
> And she that was become
> Her former beauty treble.[6]

The three schools, of course, are not always entirely separate. Tonna's pairings of morally and physically decaying sisters in both *Helen Fleetwood* and *The Wrongs of Women* demonstrate the interconnectedness of the spiritual and physical, although her impassioned pleas for mercy toward the fallen sister in each case place the moral fall within a protectionist framework. In America, Louisa May Alcott's *Work* is a testament to the power of the bodily metaphor and to the author's political and moral oscillation between a protectionist and a feminist stance. In the course of the book, Christie, the heroine, moves through a series of jobs; she is in turn a servant, an actress, a laundress, a governess, a companion, a seamstress, a florist and (after her marriage and widowhood) a feminist speaker and a philanthropist. After each experience the job is assessed in terms of Christie's physical appearance. Her transition from the morally suspect job of actress to the far more respectable role of governess is marked by a long symbolic illness. She emerges as governess with a face "refined" by sickness:

> The frank eyes had a softer shadow in their depths, the firm lips smiled less often, but when it came the smile was the sweeter for the gravity that went before, and in her voice there was a new undertone of the subtle music called sympathy, which steals into the heart and nestles there.[7]

The progression from servant to philanthropist marks and transfigures Christie's body; her stint as a laundress is pivotal in the development of a metaphor of physical and spiritual cleansing that at once erases the body by its purification and foregrounds it as it emphasizes hard physical labor.

The shared use of the body metaphor in the depiction of women's work by writers of all political persuasions is a symptom of both the strengths and weaknesses of the Victorian feminist position. Carol DuBois and Linda Gordon argue that mainstream Victorian feminism, with its emphasis on women's sexual victimization, was limited to the protection of the female body from danger.[8] I would argue further that mainstream Victorian feminism was entirely defined by the body and shaped by its contours, as its rhetoric on work clearly reveals. This position does, of course, have its strengths: the close, almost obsessive link between feminist thought and women's bodies makes it almost impossible for this brand of feminism to be overly cerebral or "irrelevant"—charges that are consistently levelled at some elements of twentieth-century feminist theory.

Compressed into one idiom—the female body—Victorian discussions of women's work are both limited and powerful. Their use of self-consciously figurative language allows them to speak the unspeakable richly and subversively. Work marks the body, making it representable, marked, remarkable. With their use of traditional metaphoric devices, Victorian authors opened secret passages for the reintroduction of women's bodies into texts that had, on the surface, cleansed themselves of such presences. In the face of taboo and absence, Victorian writers of all sorts of texts created a presence that was all the stronger for appearing not to exist.

The Embodiment of Work in Fiction

The terms of the debate over work were constantly being set and reshaped in the Victorian novel. Anna Jameson's complaint in 1846 that, "After all that has been written, sung, and said of women, one has the perception that neither in prose nor in verse has she ever appeared as a laborer" (Neff, p. 13) is valid for much of the Victorian canon. Although, according to Jameson, two million women worked outside the home by mid-century (Neff, p. 11), heroines of canonical Victorian novels rarely hold jobs, or, if they do, are even more rarely depicted in the act of working. Like sex and eating, women's work is carried on in the lacunae of the text; like sex and eating, its intimate connection with women's bodies consecrates it as taboo. We see Jane Eyre teach Adele a lesson only once in the novel in which she figures; the important action of *Jane Eyre* takes place when Mrs. Fairfax has begged a holiday for Adele, or when Rochester commands Jane to come to him after hours. Dorothea Brooke, who spends much of *Middlemarch* trying to do useful work, is full of plans for cottages but never executes a single one; in the end this labor is left for the slightly contemptible Sir James to finish. Dinah Morris begins *Adam Bede* with a vocation, but gives it up to bear children. Mary Garth is frequently on the verge of leaving home to work as a governess, but never makes it as far as the door. Little Dorrit is seen working almost as infrequently as she is seen eating; both activities take place in dark corners, away from the narrative eye.

Jenny Wren in *Our Mutual Friend* is a complex figure in this context; her sewing, for instance, is depicted in some detail. Her affliction seems, however, to set her apart from other heroines. Jenny's work and sexual desires, her plans for the "Him" who will carry her off, are treated with a mixture of pathos and irony that makes Jenny an exception to most rules of female representation. The carefully allegorical nature of her work also allows a "safe" rhetorical place for the depiction of her work and body.

Victorian noncanonical and marginally canonical[9] texts do, however, give us a more explicit picture of women working. Anne Bronte's Agnes Grey works far harder as a governess than does Jane Eyre; the novel is packed with detail about Agnes' daily trials with the children she teaches. Agnes' body figures prominently in the minute descriptions of a typical working day:

> [Mary Ann] apparently preferred rolling on the floor to any other amusement. Down she would drop like a leaden weight; and when I, with great difficulty, had succeeded in rooting her thence, I still had to hold her up with one arm, while with the other I held the book from which she was to read or spell her lessons. As the dead weight of the big girl of six became too heavy for one arm to bear, I transferred it to the other; or, if both were weary of the burden I carried her to a corner.[10]

The toll of work on Agnes' body is carefully depicted throughout the novel. The narrator herself seems self-conscious about the detail with which she tells her story, claiming she has

> . . . not enumerated half the vexatious propensities of my pupils, or half the troubles resulting from my heavy responsibilities, for fear of trespassing on the reader's patience; as perhaps I have already done　　　　　　　　　　　(*Agnes Grey*, p. 62).

Early critics of *Agnes Grey* seem to echo Anne's uneasiness with detail. An 1847 review of the novel explained that *Agnes Grey* is "a tale of a governess who undergoes much that is the real bond of a governess's endurance; but the new victim's trials are of a more ignoble quality than those which await Jane Eyre."[11] Even Charlotte Bronte seemed to hint at the overly mimetic or literal quality of her sister's work; in a letter to W. S. Williamson, after a lengthy discussion of Emily's genius, she effectively dismisses Anne's novel by focussing on its reflective rather than its creative powers: "*Agnes Grey* is the mirror of the mind of the writer."[12] Whereas work is almost always overtly metaphorized in Jane Eyre—for example, in her struggle to be independent of Rochester when she leaves his money behind—it makes up the body of *Agnes Grey*. The condescension with which the novel is frequently treated seems to turn on the issue of its pedantic literalness, its literary "trespass" in reproducing the "ignoble" realities of women's work and physical experience.

Charlotte Tonna's scrupulous attention to the details of women's work places her not only outside the canon, but outside fiction as well. She defined her own work and her own literary territory as nonfiction, although all of her books recast her observations of factory life as the life stories of fictional heroines. In self-consciously trying to reject metaphor and euphemism and replacing them with minutely detailed descriptions of machinery, working conditions, and working-class homes, she highlights and delimits the perceived choice between high literary forms and the realistic depiction of women's work.

Predictably, Elizabeth Gaskell, perched on the edge of the British canon, occupies an ambiguous place in relation to women's work. Caught between canonical silence and the busy detail of writers like Tonna, her novels both are and are not about work. Although her social novels deal almost exclusively with working-class women, her two most developed working-class heroines, Mary Barton and Ruth, are in some sense outside their class. Ruth has the instincts of a lady from the beginning of the novel, and Mary Barton is saved from the factory work in which her peers and relatives take part by her father, who considers it morally dangerous for young women. Although we do see Ruth working as a dressmaker's apprentice at the beginning of the novel, her experiences in the shop along with her subsequent sexual fall form part of her past her friends try to conceal. We never actually see Mary at work as a dressmaker; we see instead, in great detail, her domestic preparations for her father's comfort when *he* comes home from work. Mary's work and body are thus domesticated; dressmaking is not, for her, the fall into physical vanity that it is for many of the women discussed below.

Victorian culture, of course, made many distinctions between various types of women's work, and these distinctions are with some modifications reflected in the novels of the period. Although they all participate in framing a physical metaphor, they find different places within it. The following sections will consider the hobbies of leisure-class heroines, jobs for "decayed gentlewomen," and working-class occupations as they are embodied in and embody Victorian culture and fiction.

Leisure-Class Heroines: Bodies and Hobbies

Because the novel of the period deals so widely with the leisure class, it is not surprising that the biggest category of women's "work" is the loosely defined filling-up of time of the leisure-class heroine. The Victorian novel's wide empty spaces, those long periods of time in which action is virtually suspended and heroines wait for lovers to take them to perhaps larger spaces of their own, are at least partially filled up by the heroine's desire to "do something." Despite the seeming passivity of these women as they drift through hours, days, years, and pages, both novelists and essayists of the period present the heroine as participating in a violent physical struggle with time. According to Craik, young ladies "murder time," while, according to Florence Nightingale, time is the murderer and the young lady the victim. In a series of images no doubt inspired by her medical experience, Nightingale compares typical feminine "occupations" to disease and injury:

> And what is it to be "read aloud to"? The most miserable exercise of the human intellect. Or rather is it any exercise at all? It is like lying on one's back, with one's hands tied and having liquid poured down one's throat. Worse than that, because suffocation would immediately ensue and put a stop to this operation. But no suffocation would stop the other   (Nightingale, p. 34).

Nightingale goes on to elaborate upon the image by claiming that illness is the only excuse for a woman to take time for herself and to control it:

> A married woman was heard to wish that she could break a limb that she might have a little time for herself. Many take advantage of the fear of "infection" to do the same   (Nightingale, p. 34).

Novels of the period reflect leisure-class women's struggle with time. Perhaps the most famous extended time metaphor in the Victorian canon is Dickens' *Dombey and Son*, in which from the first to the last pages the characters come to terms with their own mortality to the chiming of the novel's many clocks. Almost buried in this novel of capitalist expansion and criminal intrigue, Florence Dombey watches time go by and cannot control it. Alone in her father's empty house after her brother's death, she can only stare at the wall and watch the golden river, which represents time for her, flow by. While her father and her future lover engage themselves with time by busying themselves with expansionist adventures, Florence sews at home to a different kind of time that is

measured on the one hand by her memories of her dead mother
and brother, and on the other by improbable fantasies of her father's return. In the meantime, suspended between memory and
fantasies of the future, she "works":

> Then she gained heart to look upon the work with which her fin-
> gers had been busy by (her brother's) side on the sea-shore; and
> thus it was not very long before she took to it again . . . and
> sitting in a window, near her mother's picture; in the unused
> room so long deserted, wore away the thoughtful hours.[13]

The image of Florence at her unnamed work, wearing away the
time until the men she loves draw her out of her suspended state,
reverberates throughout the Victorian canon where women sew on
unnamed garments, do unnamed and unspecified "work," to fill up
the time before the entrance of the hero.

Victorian heroines employ various strategies to fill time. Perhaps
because the very blankness of their time is, for the most part,
caused by the absence of a lover, even their "work" is overlaid with
sexual connotations; it occupies a place between girlhood and marriage and functions as a displacement of sexual desire. Emma
Woodhouse, who boasts that she does not have to marry because
of her many "independent resources," and who looks to a single
future as being full of employment—"If I draw less, I shall read
more; if I give up music, I shall take up carpet work"—actually
spends her time making misguided matches for other people.[14]
Knightley's early warning about the impropriety of matchmaking

> Your time has been properly and delicately spent, if you have
> been endeavoring for the last four years to bring about this mar-
> riage. A worthy employment for a young lady's mind
> (*Emma*, p. 12).

reveals the sexual nature of Emma's primary occupation. She does
not give up matchmaking until the minute Knightley proposes.
Emma, who uses even her feminine accomplishments, like portrait
painting, toward vaguely immodest ends, is a precursor of later
Victorian heroines whose occupations and accomplishments are
used at best as time killers and at worst as excuses or euphemisms
for sexual activity.

Perhaps the most universal pastime among these leisure-class heroines is walking. Lonely, often physically gruelling walks, through oppressively familiar territory are sometimes the only outlet for a heroine's physicality. Caroline Helstone roams the Yorkshire moors until "she is ready to drop," thinking of Robert and of the fact that he has no leisure to think of her. Austen's Emma and other more enterprising heroines use walks as a means of social control by planning excursions to places of interest. The younger Bennett sisters in *Pride and Prejudice* walk daily into town in the hopes of chance encounter with a red-coated officer. Maggie Tulliver takes restless and ultimately compromising walks into the Red Deeps, where she is followed by Philip. Walks are a "daily necessity" to Molly Gibson; she is out scrambling to pick blackberries while Roger proposes to Cynthia. The heroine's tremendous physical energy, translated into a few short sentences in the vast verbal landscape that makes up the Victorian novel, is often lost or buried. The energy and the restlessness, however, are almost always seen in sexual terms and are translated into romantic and sexual events. Aimless as the heroine's walking sometimes appears to be, it beats out a path toward marriage and physical fulfillment; it is an important effort on the part of the heroines to influence the direction of the novel and of their lives.

Sewing, perhaps the most common feminine occupation, embodies many of the same contradictions as walking. While on the surface it is a safe, dainty, and appropriately feminine way of filling up time and hope chests, sewing is also a way of repressing and, therefore, implicitly admitting unlawful and dangerous sexual need. Gilbert and Gubar have shown that Victorian novels are full of "needlers," or women whose power over the needle reflects a larger power to manipulate and control the "web" of other characters' destinies. Rosamond's exquisite sewing in *Middlemarch*, Pauline's weaving of her husband's and lover's hair together in *Villette*, Zoraide's knitting in *The Professor* are all, according to Gilbert and Gubar, reflections of feminine desire to control the text and the men they ensnare in their carefully crafted webs.[15]

For other heroines like Maggie Tulliver, Caroline Helstone, and Aurora Leigh, however, sewing represents not so much a desire or an ability to control others, but a way of repressing and controlling the self. Sewing, for these three heroines, means the sacrifice of physical self and the repression of bodily urges. In the three works in which these heroines appear, sewing is the tiny and fragile channel into which their creativity and their sexual energies must be poured to maintain feminine decorum. The seams into which Victorian heroines channel their desire become seams or scars in the text; while leisure-class sewers try to make both bodies and stitches invisible, seams, however dainty, mark the tissue of the novel and produce a trace of the heroine's physical presence.

The paraphernalia of sewing, especially needles and scissors, take on a sinister connotation in *The Mill on the Floss*. Even Lucy, the paragon of femininity, will find scissors dangerous. In her happy moments of courtship, before Maggie's arrival on the scene, she flirts with Stephen over a pair of scissors:

> "My scissors, please, if you can renounce the great pleasure of persecuting my poor Minny." The foolish scissors have slipped too far over the knuckles, it seems, and Hercules holds out his entrapped fingers hopelessly. "Confound the scissors! The oval lies the wrong way. Please draw them off for me."[16]

The playful irony that characterizes the narrator's attitude toward Lucy gives way to something graver here: the scissors evolve from a plaything into both a harbinger of separation and a manacle.

If the scissors are damaging to Lucy, the needle is fatal to Maggie's physical desires. When Stephen sings, releasing in her a flood of inappropriate passion for music and for Stephen himself, she bends assiduously over her sewing. The music repeatedly causes her to drop her work, but she returns to it grimly, "making false stitches and pricking her fingers with much perseverance" (*Mill*, p. 367). The seeming insignificance of Maggie's pain, these little finger pricks, is in itself a form of repression: acute and real as Maggie's suffering is, it is domesticated and tamed, trivialized in its metaphorization into pinpricks. Many critics have suggested that the final flood that ends *The Mill on the Floss* is a projection of Maggie's physical desires which, repressed throughout the novel, come back to engulf her. The tiny, feminine drops of blood on Maggie's sewing surely stand in ironic contrast to the water of the Floss as symbols of her repressed nature. Maggie's blood, trivialized by the feminine image, is shed exceedingly small along the seams of her "plain sewing."

If Maggie becomes a sewer to contain her own desire, Caroline

Helstone of *Shirley* becomes herself a fabric, cut, shaped, and sewn by her jealous cousin Hortense. Hortense smothers Caroline in cloth as she forces her to sew; she both insists that Caroline perform the endless task of darning stockings the "Belgian way" and covers her cousin's body in cloth, forcing her to make herself a fichu to cover her curls and a Belgian neckcloth to disguise the sensuality of her throat and shoulders. By forcing Caroline to sew her own coverings, Hortense "needles" her into submissive femininity, shaping her body and desire to the cloth she imposes on her. Darning a single pair of stockings takes Caroline three years; it is useless labor that serves only to channel Caroline's energy into appropriately feminine activity.

As *Shirley* proceeds and Caroline is banished from her cousins' farm by her uncle, the "Jew-basket" replaces the half-finished stockings as a symbol of feminine futility:

> It ought to be explained in passing for the benefit of those who are not "au fait" to the mysteries of the "Jew-basket" and "Missionary-basket" that these "meubles" are willow-repositories, of the capacities of a good-sized family clothes basket, dedicated to the purpose of conveying from house to house a monster collection of pin-cushions, needle-books, card-racks, workbags, articles of infant wear . . . made by the willing or reluctant hands of Christian ladies of the parish, and sold perforce to the heathenish gentlemen thereof, at prices unblushingly exorbitant. The proceeds of such compulsory sales are applied to the conversion of the Jews, the seeking up of the ten missing tribes, or to the regeneration of the interesting coloured population of the globe.[17]

Like articles prepared by Lucy and Maggie for the church bazaar, the contents of the Jew-basket are both symbols of wasted feminine energy and ritual props for courtship and sexual interaction. The selling of handiwork at "unblushingly exorbitant" prices is a social and sexual act in which both Caroline and Maggie are reluctant and embarrassed to participate. Caroline hates the Jew-basket and shudders when it is her turn to fill it, while Maggie becomes uncomfortable and almost sullen when she is declared the belle of the bazaar and men flock to buy the dressing gowns featured at her stall.

In *Aurora Leigh*, sewing and traditional women's work take on an even more sinister cast. Aurora makes the connection between

her body and fabric explicit, "suffering" her aunt to "prick me to
a pattern with her pin, fibre from fibre."[18] The female body and
mind, then, become symbols of their own wasted energies. Although Aurora rejects needlework for writing and comments explicitly on both the uselessness and symbolic importance of sewing, "by the way, / The works of women are symbolical / We sew,
sew, prick our fingers, dull our sight, / Producing what? / A pair of
slippers, sir" (*Aurora Leigh*, Bk. 1, l. 456), she inflates the importance of the same work she scorns by translating it into epic form.
She gives over several lines of this ambitious epic to the description
of an embroidered shepherdess, to whom, having "mistook the
silks," she gave pink eyes to match her slippers. Even mistakes are
epicized in this faithful rendering of female experience; female occupations, however, trivialized by the culture, are—to use Browning's idiom—the fabric of the poem. As the epic unfolds, finger
pricks and dulled sight from sewing conflate into larger images of
female bleeding and vision. The miniature pinpricks suffered by
Maggie in *The Mill on the Floss* are inflated into structural images of blood and bleeding linked explicitly to female sexuality.[19]

The third major occupation for young ladies and leisure-class
heroines alike was philanthropy, or, in a looser sense, the helping
of other people. Although philanthropy is, on the surface, only an
extension of the heroine's familial role as nurturer, even this "safe
and becoming occupation for women" has its roots in a desire for
physical expression and leaves its marks or scars on the body.

In Gaskell's *Wives and Daughters*, Molly, identified as the female "worker" of the family, practices the most harmless and pri-
vatized forms of philanthropy. All her good "works" are for the
benefit of her family, or those who will eventually become part of
it. She steps outside the home only to nurse the family at the Hall
into which she will marry by the end of the book, and to protect
her sister Cynthia by negotiating for the return of letters to an ex-
lover.

Molly is symbolically and literally stained by her wanderings out
of the house. When Roger is at Molly's home proposing to the
useless and ornamental Cynthia, Molly is out picking berries for
her stepsister, tearing her dress, and significantly staining her hands,
face, and dress with juice. When she goes out to meet Cynthia's
ex-lover, it is she who is accused of having a romantic liaison with

him; even her father, Molly's staunchest supporter, begins to doubt his daughter's purity. Finally, when she goes to the Hall to make peace between family members there, Mrs. Gibson hints at the impropriety of staying there without a chaperone. This puts a constraint on Molly's behavior to Roger and sets up a barrier between them.

Even the puritanical Dorothea Brooke expresses her relations to her work in physical terms. Despite her constant attempts to mortify her flesh by giving up riding and marrying a man without physical attractions, her very philanthropy has its physical roots and expression. In explaining her reasons for planning cottages, her language is revealing in its intense physicality. Dorothea maintains that rich people should be "beaten out of their beautiful houses with a scourge of small cords"[20] for not involving themselves in the housing problems of the local poor. Celia's astute comment that Dorothea "likes giving up" speaks both to the physical nature of the guilt Dorothea experiences and to the sensual pleasures involved in erasing it.

Elizabeth Gaskell's Margaret Hale, the heroine of *North and South*, explicitly links philanthropy and the body in a more positive way. The very act of stepping outside her door into the streets of Milton makes her feel and look healthier despite the town's dirt and impure air:

> Margaret went out heavily and unwillingly enough. But the length of a street—yes, the air of a Milton street—cheered her young blood before she reached her first turning. Her step grew lighter, her lips redder. She began to take notice . . .[21]

There is so much work to be done in Milton, so many chances for usefulness, that Margaret cannot help growing healthy and interested. Paradoxically, Margaret's symptoms of rosy health mimic those she had seemingly left behind her with the air of the pastoral Helstone.

Margaret's "work" in Milton does not stop at the traditional visiting of the poor. She steps further outside her home and literally into the public eye when she defends John from the strikers by throwing her body between him and a flying clog. Margaret at once defends her action *as* work, transfiguring what could be interpreted as an erotic moment.

If I saved one blow, one cruel, angry action that might otherwise
have been committed, I did a woman's work. Let them insult my
maiden pride as they will—I walk pure before God

(*North and South*, p. 191).

Margaret's careful de-erotization of what could be a revelation of
sexual desire paradoxically reveals the erotic nature of this—and
other—"women's work." The act of making her body public causes
her to swoon and bleed and John to confess his love for her. John's
mother complains that Margaret has "thrown herself" at her son
in a sexual manner. Margaret's scar, which she manages to hide by
deft feminine manipulations of her hair, has obvious symbolic
weight. She has trespassed by enlarging the definition of woman's
work and must bear the physical and psychic scars that result from
her action.

The Victorian Governess: Between Two Bodies

The language of sexual fall in these novels of domestic life shows
how precarious a hold these heroines had on the title of young
lady. At any moment a step outside the home might plunge them
into a net of extended metaphors that could undermine their claim
to strict purity. More uncertain than their individual conduct,
however, was the economic position of their family. Young ladies
who lost their fortunes in the social and economic upheavals that
accompanied industrialization were often forced out of their homes
into the role of governess. Governesses and young ladies are linked
in Victorian fiction by the possibility of an alternative narrative;
every leisure-class heroine, given the possibility of financial disaster,
is a possible governess. The novels of the period are, in fact, filled
with heroines on the verge of becoming governesses who are saved
at the last minute by marriage. Because the distinctions between
governess and young lady are so fuzzy, the fall into governessing so
eminently possible, the governess becomes the heroine's shadow-
double, the figure in muted grey or brown who follows the gaily
dressed heroine back and forth from church visits to the poor and
who is always one step behind her in her progress through the
novel.

In many ways the governess was not only indistinguishable from
the young lady, but the epitome of young ladyhood itself. Victo-

rian governesses were supposed to be a veritable storehouse of feminine accomplishments; advertisements for governesses frequently demanded that, at a young age, she be in command of everything from ballroom dancing to the use of globes.[22] The connection between the perfect governess and the ideal young lady was satirized in a letter from a young man to his sister in which he answers her request to find her a governess by claiming that if he ever found such perfection in a woman he would marry her and not send her on to his sister (Neff, p. 160). Elizabeth Eastlake attests to the uneasy distinction between governess and young lady: "The real definition of a governess, in the English sense, is a being who is our equal in birth, manners and education but our inferior in worldly wealth."[23] The governess is genetically a young lady, dressed in the trappings of a working woman.

Many nineteenth-century novels with conventionally happy endings turn on the possibility of young lady heroines slipping out of their secure class position into that of a governess. Governessing is a bleak possibility for Caroline Helstone, Jane Fairfax, Gwendolyn Harleth, and Mary Garth, while Diana and Mary Rivers teach for a short time offstage only to resume their positions as young ladies. Because becoming a governess is always presented as the alternative to a happy marriage, the role of governess assumes, for most of these heroines, the symbolic weight of sexual repression. To Caroline, the possibility of becoming a governess is a "harsh but effective cure" for her unrequited passion (*Shirley*, p. 246). Grace Crawley of *The Last Chronicle of Barset* uses the school where she teaches as a sanctuary against the temptation of admitting her love for the wealthy Captain Grantly. The "cure," to use Caroline's word, is only effected through the sacrifice of the desire for love; when Jane Fairfax bitterly calls the governess trade a "trade in human flesh," she could well be talking about the sacrifice of her own more fleshly desires (*Emma*, p. 284). Perhaps the only exception in the equation of governessing with sexual repression is Jane Eyre who, as we will see later, turns the body metaphor inside out to derive sexual power from her ambiguous class position.

If governesses hover between two class alliances, they also hover between the two bodies prescribed for women and described earlier in this chapter—the delicate frame of the leisure-class lady and the robust body of the working-class woman. In the more romantic governess novels of the early part of the century and in the more gothic treatments of the governess theme later on, the position of governess, metaphorically speaking, is no more than a temporary disguise which it is the duty of both the hero and the reader to pierce. Underneath the subdued costume of the governess is the delicate and sensitive body of the leisure-class heroine. Lady Blessington's early *The Governess* and Mrs. Wood's sensation novel *East Lynne* use their governess' delicate bodies as an indication of their true class position. In contrast, in perhaps the most complex rendering of the governess motif, *Jane Eyre* depicts a heroine caught between two bodies; at various times in the novel she tries on the body of a leisure-class heroine and of a worker, but realizes she can completely fit into neither. By the end of the century, in George Gissing's attempt at social realism, *The Odd Women*, the governess has moved to the other end of the class spectrum to claim the body of a worker. The shift in the political position of the governess is accompanied by a shift in cultural perceptions of her physical self.

Perhaps the paradigmatic instance of the governess as lady in disguise is *East Lynne*, in which the disguise is literal. Isabel Vane's fall forces her away from her home; she can only return as governess to her own children. The only difference between Isabel Vane and Madame Vine is a name, a disguise, a fall. In her case, of course, the fall is sexual; in the case of Clara Mortuant of Lady Blessington's *The Governess* it is financial. Since a financial fall may be reversed, Clara can reestablish herself as heroine and throw away her disguise by the end of the novel.

The Governess is a particularly good example of how thin the veneer of "governess" is. Clara's true ladyhood, always expressed in physical terms, is only temporarily obscured by the superficial trappings of her position. Throughout the novel, Clara's physical sensations, her body itself, are obviously that of a young lady. Vulgarity in any form affects her physically. When she goes down to dessert at the home of her first employer,

> . . . the mingled odors of soup, fish, flesh, pineapple and melon, struck most disagreeably on her olfactory nerves, as did the blaze of several lamps on her optic ones, as she entered the dining room.[24]

Almost the same anatomical formula is used in describing her reaction to a public street:

> Her auracular faculties were stunned by the din of so many rough
> voices, and her olfactory ones no less disagreeably assailed by the
> mingled odors of spiritous liquors and tobacco (*Governess*, p. 20).

Clara's assertions of ladyhood are almost always expressed in terms
of food. Her first struggle with her charges is to prevent them from
fighting over mutton and getting their dresses greasy; her second is
to get a glass of ice water sent up to her with dinner instead of
beer. By the end of the first day of fast-paced coded action, when
both servants and children realize she is a lady, Betsey, the nursery
maid, sends up "a nice meal with iced water, napkins, and finger
glasses" instead of the messy dinner tray she sent to previous governesses (*Governess*, p. 42). Clara's delicacy, predictably enough,
is contrasted with the vulgarity of her employers and their friends.
Mrs. Williamson looks like a "radish" in red silk and emeralds,
while an unnamed lady in yellow satin "tucks into the vol-au-vent"
pastry "in famous style" (*Governess*, p. 38).

Both the reader and the hero, Mr. Seymour, easily penetrate the
disguise of "poor dependent" and see the young lady beneath. By
the end of the novel, Clara throws off the disguise and reveals herself once more to be an heiress. Like Jane Eyre, she cannot marry
her lover from a position of poverty; her young ladyhood must be
established as an entity separate from anything Seymour could
confer: it occupies the private space of her own body.

If reading *The Governess* is an act of penetrating a thin disguise, reading *Jane Eyre* is a veritable masquerade in which neither
the reader nor the character can consistently tell the difference between mask and reality. Throughout the novel both Jane and
Rochester try on a series of disguises and personae that grow more
and more complex at the point of apparent unveiling. Jane's "discovery" that Rochester is the gypsy, for instance, only complicates
matters and generates new questions about their respective roles.
For Jane, even more than Rochester, the novel is a series of costume fittings that focus on the central contradictions between heroine and dependent.

Throughout the first part of the novel the people in Jane's world try to mold her body into that of a dependent. The public display of body at Lowood begins a series of episodes that define Jane in this way. Jane herself uses this identity, this body, as a way of trying to repress inappropriate feelings for Rochester; in an effort to conquer her jealousy of Blanche, Jane resorts to the device of painting their two opposing portraits and labelling them according to class. Blanche is "an accomplished young lady of rank" and Jane "a governess, disconnected, poor and plain."[25] In creating the two portraits, Jane has replicated the two bodies that served as alternatives for Victorian women. Her implicit equation of aristocracy and physical beauty makes the connection between class and the body quite clear. The two portraits and the two socioanatomical constructions they represent dominate the rest of the novel, serving as reference points in Jane's physical and emotional journey.

As the novel progresses, it becomes increasingly clear that Jane fits entirely into neither portrait, neither body. Like Lucy Snowe in *Villette* who must learn to reject both the Cleopatra and the series of bland paintings that comprise "la vie d'une femme," Jane must come to terms with the fact that she lives outside both bodies. Just as she is not completely a dependent—Rochester's love for her tells her that—she is not a leisure-class heroine. When Rochester makes the mistake of dressing Jane "in borrowed plumes" for the first wedding, he is committing the larger error of assuming her body is now like Blanche's, to be dressed in the trappings of young ladyhood (*Jane Eyre*, p. 314).

Jane's ambiguous bodily position is both potentially transformative and dangerous. Rochester's assumption that Jane has *no* body, no physical needs, discussed in the previous chapter, is demeaning and potentially fatal to Jane. The flexibility of her position, however, allows for a new bodily language which she and Rochester invent between them. Because Jane does not belong to either body, physical sexuality can appear, as it were, in the gap between the two paintings. Rochester can speak of the stirring that ties their ribs together, can go back to Eden and to prelapsarian classlessness for his diction, can stress the body, before moral or financial fall as a source of his love.

Jane's final position vis-à-vis Rochester is carefully charted in physical terms. As they leave the garden in the final scene, Jane is both Rochester's prop and guide; she is able to support him only because she is so much "lower" than he. Jane's body is Rochester's main support, but it is a support and strength that comes out of relative weakness. The perfect balance of this ending is perfectly physical. Jane's new "work" as Rochester's wife demands the use of a powerful physical icon.

The movement of the governess out of the body of the young lady and into the body of the worker is completed in *The Odd Women*. Virginia's and Agnes' attempts at delicacy, their pretense that one tiny meal a day is enough for them, is depicted as both pathetic and self-destructive. Virginia, the governess, is described in excruciatingly physical detail:

> The elder (now five-and-thirty) tended to corpulence, the result of a sedentary life: she had round shoulders and very short legs. Her face would not have been disagreeable except for its spoilt complexion: the homely features, if health had but rounded and coloured them, would have expressed pleasantly enough the gentleness and sincerity of her character. Her cheeks were loose, puffy and permanently of the hue which is produced by cold; her forehead generally had a few pimples; her shapeless chin lost itself in two or three fissures.[26]

Descriptions like this, which abound in the book, put the sisters' abused bodies on display for the readers much in the same way Rhoda Nunn wants the bodies of young women forced into teaching to be displayed before the British public. When Monica complains about how hard it is for young ladies to "get a place," Rhoda replies:

> "And I wish it were harder. I wish girls fell down and died of hunger in the streets, instead of creeping into their garrets and the hospitals. I should like to see their dead bodies piled up in some open place for the crowd to stare at" (*Odd Women*, p. 97).

The display of these dead bodies is the final public act and the final act of moving the governess or teacher from the house into the street. In *The Odd Women*, governesses' bodies are the bodies of other female workers, to be piled indiscriminately before the public gaze.

The public display of these dead bodies marks the final transition of the governess from young lady to worker. As Gissing, through Rhoda, wrenches the governess out of her garret and her unrealistic class affiliation, he proclaims her a "public woman" whose body must be stared at, read, and interpreted. By the end of Rhoda's speech she has torn away even the most treasured trappings of young ladyhood: family, home, privacy, and modesty disappear as class disguise is removed, revealing the body beneath.

Rhoda's call for women to bring their bodies out of hiding has its other, more positive side. Once euphemism has been lifted from the discussion of women's bodies, there is more room for the bodies of working women to grow strong and healthy. Rhoda and Mary's work contributes to their physical well-being; both look younger than their years, and Rhoda in particular is consistently described in terms of physical strength. In a reversal of the traditional Victorian theme, her strength is in turn eroticized, so that Evrard feels the movement of Rhoda's well-developed hand muscles with intense sexual pleasure. He is equally attracted to her stamina in their walking tour of the lake country. Feminine asexuality, delicacy, and lack of appetite are exposed as sham when Virginia falls eagerly on a piece of beef at Rhoda's house after explaining that she is a vegetarian.

Working-Class Women: A Public Body

If the work of young ladies and governesses is depicted in bodily terms, it should be no surprise that the work of working-class women—already perceived in the Victorian idiom as coarser and more animalistic—should make use of the same, and stronger, language. Most exposés of the plight of the working-class woman concentrate either on the physical toll of hard work or on moral problems translated into physical terms. The three options for fictional working-class women seem to be prostitution, severe illness, or death. The consequences of hard physical work stretch out in only two directions from the focal point of the heroine's body.

Even more than her leisure-class sister, the working-class woman was, by mid-century, a body to be studied and commented upon. Henry Mayhew's accounts of working-class women are by no means the only such studies produced by Victorian culture. T. J. Edelstein's recent article on the iconology of the Victorian seamstress illustrates the cultural fascination with women of the lower classes, while the diaries of Arthur Munby reproduce the Victorian working-class woman as object for scholarly scrutiny and sexual fantasy. His detailed physical descriptions of working-class women reveal a man obsessed by laboring women as bodies:

> Her head of course was bare; her hair had been drawn tight behind her ears and knotted behind, but was all rough and rumpled and adust, with carrying the sacks. She wore an old gown of nameless material, sodden with laborious sweat; her broad breast (for she was a tall, strongly built wench of twenty or so) was loosely covered with a red and orange kerchief, the two ends hanging in a knot.[27]

His description ends by distancing the observer from the subject: "So much for that sight" (Hiley, p. 11). Typically, Munby made use of the two aspects of the body discussed earlier by pairing the moral and the physical. In expressing his hopes for future study, he claims: "If I had the means, I would investigate, being now old enough to do so without misconstruction, the moral and physical statistics of laboring women all over the world" (Hiley, p. 11).

Victorian observers of the "laboring classes" made some distinction between urban and rural working women. London and factory towns like Manchester were seen in both the fiction and the non-fiction of the time as centers of moral and physical decay. Interestingly, American factory owners tried to distance themselves from the "degradation" they associated with "the manufacturing cities of Europe" by espousing a form of protectionist capitalism.[28] Mill owners in the town of Lowell, Massachusetts, built boardinghouses for their female employees and imposed a curfew and other regulations to insure a moral purity. They boasted that these houses were "under the charge of respectable women [and included] every provision for religious worship" (Dublin, p. 77).

Novelists like Charlotte Tonna used London and other cities as catalysts for moral and physical degeneration. In *The Wrongs of Women*, which follows the career of two sisters sent from the country to London to learn a trade, one dies of consumption and the other is seduced and takes to the streets; the process of moral decay in Frances parallels the physical decay in Ann.

Ann, a milliner's apprentice, begins her job with an excited admiration for London and everything it stands for. Her sickly fellow-apprentices seem beautiful to her; hard work is not only translated into physical description but into a masochistic aesthetic of female beauty:

> She imagines that universal air of languor, that absence of healthful glow, that reed-like attenuation of figure, to be the result of London polish. . . . She notices the long, faint, unwinding tresses that depend from the heads of these young milliners, and wonders if her own crisp, elastic curls will ever hang so droopingly.[29]

The words "faint," "depend," and "long" refer metonymically to the workers' situations as well as to their physical appearance in this physiognomist's translation of work into looks.

Predictably and ironically, after Ann has been on the job for a year, after she has been denied the delicate food, fresh air, and exercise she was so used to at home, her appearance is transfigured into this parody of feminine delicacy:

> Poor Ann! The slim, bowed figure and the tresses of thin, loose, flossy hair, bear little vestige of the plump contour and bright rich curls that marked the young girl . . . twelve months since
> (Tonna, p. 405).

Ann's illness and the conditions that produced it are frequently described in morally charged terms. Tonna speaks of the "impure breath" of the young girls, and concludes that "the air respired by them must become foetid to a degree at once loathsome and injurious to the yet healthy victims" (Tonna, p. 404).

Frances is allowed more air and exercise, but that in itself becomes a problem as she is too often in the streets and exposed to coarse language. Just as Ann's physical decay is accompanied by images of moral disease, so Frances' moral fall is indicated by physical symptoms:

> Frances agreeably surprises her father by the comparative healthfulness of her appearance, and the activity of her step; but in one respect she is more changed than Ann. Her childishness is succeeded by the aspect of more years than she has really numbered
> (Tonna, p. 409).

In the still more pious *Helen Fleetwood*, Tonna develops her joint attack on working conditions and the feminine aesthetic. The two issues are most closely connected in Tonna's description of one of the young girls in Helen's extended family, who has been working in a factory since she was an infant. The description applies traditional metaphors of female beauty to a girl who is obviously both a moral and physical wreck. This disjunction between the subject and the means of the description, the tenor and vehicle of the metaphor, isolates the vehicle and forces the reader to look at its more ludicrous and therefore sinister side:

> The third [daughter] was the spectre of a very pretty girl, whose naked arms resembled ivory wands rather than limbs of natural flesh and blood, while her hair, black as the raven's wing, thin as gossamer threads . . . falling, or rather, floating down to her very narrow shoulders, set off the deadly white of her complexion with such an effect that she seemed like one in whose veins the current of life had already ceased to circulate   (Tonna, p. 519).

The "ivory wands" and the "raven-black," "gossamer" hair that in some contexts would be signs of beauty are in this case signs of a fatal disease. Tonna links disease and traditional notions of female beauty in an autobiographical letter marked by the same mistrust of metaphor:

> [Her neighbor's child] grew up a wandlike figure, graceful and interesting, and died of decline at nineteen, while I, though not able to compare shapes with a wasp or an hour-glass, yet passed muster very fairly among human forms   (Tonna, p. 1).

The factory girl's disease is obviously moral as well; she is not only a victim but a corrupter in her turn. It is she who instigates rumors that her brother and Helen Fleetwood are engaged in an illicit correspondence, and she who first brands Helen a whore. The "letters" Helen sends to Bill are, in fact, nothing more than explanations of Biblical concepts requested by his dying sister; in the contaminated context of factory life even Biblical words can be twisted to perverse ends.

Working-class heroines stumble and fall sexually in the Victorian canon as well as in more "popular" works. Ruth, of Gaskell's novel by that name, and "Little Emily" of *David Copperfield* both occupy the same position as dressmakers' apprentices and both fall into the arms of rich seducers. Although Emily's fall is largely unexamined, Ruth's love of beauty, good looks, and physical energy are obviously the cause of her straying. Ruth's repentance follows the same metaphor of physicality and disease; she becomes a fever-nurse and dies nursing her lover through a dangerous bout of typhoid. Clearly, Ruth catches both moral and physical diseases from Bellingham; both can be said to be the cause of her death.[30]

It is probably not a coincidence that both Ruth and Little Emily are dressmakers. As Alcott hints in *Work*, dressmaking panders to female vanity by surrounding workers with "pretty things." Ruth's job allows her to enter a ballroom and to envy the dancers from her marginal position as mender of torn ballgowns. Female vanity, of course, leads to temptation, and temptation to sexual fall.

It is not, however, only the motif of female vanity that allowed the seamstress to occupy so central a place in the Victorian conscience. As T. J. Edelstein explains, the seamstress's body was depicted everywhere, in poems, articles, engravings, and wall paintings. The solitary, pathetic figure appeared on the walls of fine houses and prestigious art galleries.[31] Edelstein suggests that Victorians focussed on the seamstress because of her femininity, her helplessness, and her solitude. This analysis seems, however, to overlook the importance of female dress as a symbol. One *Punch* cartoon, entitled, "The Haunted Lady of 'The Ghost' in the Looking Glass," depicts a young lady looking in a mirror at the vision of herself in a new gown, only to see the dead figure of the young woman who presumably made the dress gazing back at her. The two women look strangely alike; the dead seamstress is merely the young lady "undressed" of her finery and her class position.[32] Like the governess, the seamstress seems at times to inhabit the body of a young lady or to *be* the body that is dressed and hidden.

The world of factory towns and large cities is obviously morally and physically corrupt in the Victorian novel. Authors as diverse as Tonna and Hardy look to the preindustrial past and to the country for an example of women's work that is healthy and pure. In both *Helen Fleetwood* and *Tess*, the heroines, in their original pastoral settings, are part of the landscape; the land around them is a physical extension of their bodies. Tonna uses landscape to describe Helen's character:

> There was nothing in [it] unusually elevated above the class to which she belonged; but it owed some of its finer fibre to the scenery of her native land   (Tonna, p. 517).

Hardy draws the link between Tess and the landscape in more overtly physical terms:

> But those of the other [female] sex were the most interesting of this company of binders, by reason of the charm that is acquired by a woman when she becomes part and parcel of outdoor nature, and is not merely set down as an object therein as at ordinary times. A field-man is a personality afield; a field-woman is a portion of the field; she has somehow lost her own margin.[33]

Like Helen Fleetwood, who in the last passage is just coming home from milking a cow, Tess is part of nature as she works. The Eden-like charm of Talbothay's dairy is further enhanced by the fact that Tess and her relationship with Angel are in complete harmony with outdoor work; their first kiss takes place as Tess is milking, their engagement articulated as they drive the milk to be shipped.

As the novel continues, however, Tess is increasingly separated from nature in her work. The climax of separation occurs in the threshing scene where the machine spits symbolic hellfire, and Alec appears through the smoke as a devil. Industrialization takes women out of nature and separates their bodies from their tasks. Tess' body has nothing to do with this second involvement with Alec, just as it has nothing to do with her work at the same point in the novel.

The pastoral innocence of agricultural work is more cynically framed in *Adam Bede*, where Hetty's butter-molding becomes a major part of her physical attraction for Arthur. Her work is explicitly eroticized, despite the innocence suggested by the purity and whiteness of the butter and cream with which she is surrounded:

> And they are the prettiest attitudes and movements into which a pretty girl is thrown in making up butter . . . tossing movements that give a charming curve to the arm, and a sideward inclination of the round white neck; little patting and rolling movements with the palm of the hand, and nice adaptations and finishings which cannot at all be effected without a great play of the pouting mouth and dark eyes.[34]

Although on one level Hetty is manipulating the scene for her own ends, her ultimate ignorance and helplessness in this affair with Arthur highlight the fact that even while working she is not so

much subject as object. Like Tess, her work renders her a point of
focus for the implied reader who is invited by the narrator to enter
Hall farm as a spy. Hetty's attitude toward work is, of course, contrasted throughout to Adam's, who derives a sense of pride and
identity from his carpentry.

Hardy and Eliot put a different moral value on the relationship
between a woman's body and her work, although both see work in
terms of the body. For Hardy, at least in *Tess*, physical desire is
natural and therefore innocent; it is society, symbolized by the
threshing machine, that is the problem.[35] In *Adam Bede*, the involvement of the body is in itself suspect; Eliot constantly compares Hetty to Dinah, who claims she forgets her body completely
as she preaches.

Although the value placed on the female body changes from
author to author, its outlines appear against a background of class.
Young lady, governess, factory worker, and field hand join to form
a socioeconomic spectrum along which women's bodies take shape.
While this chapter posits and sketches the contours of this spectrum, the next, with its focus on the woman with a vocation and
the prostitute, examines two "moments" on this spectrum where
the female body undergoes a particularly complex and problematic
process of representation.

CHAPTER III

Calling and Falling:
Vocation and Prostitution

> Yet Jenny, looking long at you,
> The woman almost fades from view.
> A cipher of man's changeless sum
> Of lust, past, present and to come,
> Is left. A riddle that one shrinks
> To challenge from the scornful sphinx.[1]

With these words the speaker of Dante Gabriel Rossetti's "Jenny" apostrophizes the sleeping prostitute who lends the poem her name. Lying stationary at the center of the poem's action and of the Victorian debate over fallen women, it would seem that Jenny's body and its concerns would dominate the poem. The speaker's strategy, however, is the erasure of Jenny's body in the very act of its representation. From the beginning of the poem a slow process of metaphorization distances both reader and speaker from her body, first by the use of conventional tropes and finally by the transfiguration of Jenny herself into a sign.

In the first stanza, where Jenny's hair is compared to "countless gold" and her eyes to "blue skies," Jenny shares the representational fate of a long series of other women; her body, or the portions of it the speaker chooses to represent and to invest with symbolic weight, is described in terms of familiar feminine tropes. The particularities of Jenny's experience, body, and position are engulfed in a litany of conventional comparisons.

As the poem progresses, the speaker begins to separate Jenny from other women, not to liberate her from cliché, but to capture

59

Dante Gabriel Rossetti, "Found," oil on canvas. With the permission of The Delaware Art Museum.

her in his own personal idiom. About halfway through the poem Jenny becomes a "book . . . half read by lightening in a dream." The speaker has already established his own identification with books in comparing his room "so full of books" with Jenny's. Jenny becomes, then, another in a series of his books, the poem and the speaker's mission a hermeneutical exercise on a silent text. The economy implicit in the speaker's hermeneutics unfolds as Jenny's hair, once "countless gold" becomes, more explicitly, a pile of guineas. Like the books, the guineas are symbols from the speaker's world; the unconscious Jenny is easily transformed from a complex individual into a system of signs the speaker can readily understand. Taken in conjunction, the twin metaphors of sex and money inscribe the speaker's sex and class on Jenny's sleeping body as surely as the names of her clients are scrawled with diamond rings upon her mirror.

It is an easy transition from text to cipher; the potentially complex and liberating possibilities of textuality evaporate as Jenny is reduced, interestingly enough, to a cipher of *male* lust. Her sexuality and her body are denied her as, like her mirror, she becomes a reflection of other people's desires, a blank page on which a series of men can write their narratives of her significance.[2] Reduced to a figure rather than a body, captured in language, her likeness taken in sleep, Jenny cannot, even if she knew the words with which to reframe the speaker's articulate rendering of experiences, offer a counternarrative. The poem ends as it begins with her silence and invisibility; there will be no awakening into language for Jenny. The poem, considered shockingly explicit in its day, is bodiless.

In the spirit of a century that likes to pair its heroines, contrasting light and dark, the spiritual and the fleshly, the angel of the house and the streetwalker, it is perhaps appropriate to speak of *Adam Bede's* Dinah Morris as Jenny's opposite. Saintly and self-denying, Dinah seems to proclaim her task to be the erasure of her own body from the text. When the attention of both the town and the reader are focussed on her during her first sermon, we are told: "she seemed as unconscious of her outward appearance as a little boy,"[3] and when Mr. Irwine asks her if she is embarrassed to be gazed at by so many men, she answers with what seems to be a parable of self-effacement:

"No, I've no room for such feelings, and I don't think people
ever take notice of that. I think sir, when God makes his presence felt through us, we are like the burning bush; Moses never
took heed of what sort of bush it was—he only saw the brightness
of the Lord"   (*Adam Bede*, p. 94).

The reference to the trope of the burning bush is meant on the
one hand to distract both Irwine and the reader from the unnamed
tenor of her metaphor, the "that" of her first sentence—her body
and her sexuality. Dinah's inflammatory rhetorical figure, however,
also has the paradoxical effect of reminding us of the sexual fires
within Dinah, thereby inscribing her body all the more firmly in
the reader's consciousness. The pun on "burning bush," hidden as
it is by the shift to Biblical trope, becomes a coded and potentially
subversive means of access to Dinah's body through its apparent
negation.

The rhetorical strategies of both *Adam Bede* and "Jenny" subvert expectation. The prostitute's body is dressed, defaced, and
erased, while the body of the young female saint is flamboyantly
inscribed. The paradox described by the opposition of these two
women's bodies stands at the center of Victorian conventions of
representation as well as of Victorian attitudes about vocation and
prostitution. It is when talking about vocation that Victorian language is at its most coded, most subversive, and most fertile. Depictions of the prostitute, on the other hand, are strangely sexless.
While vocation allowed for the free and fertile play of codes, the
subject of prostitution seems only to have stifled Victorian representational creativity. While, as I have discussed in the previous
chapter, the prostitute as metaphor lent sexual richness to other
forms of women's work, the Victorian attempt to literalize the
prostitute's experience, to speak of her as "real," muffles and erases
the very sexuality that lends such richness to depictions of more
conventional forms of women's work. This chapter will focus on
the woman with a vocation and the prostitute, pairing them and
their bodies according to the paradox of Victorian representation,
as Jenny and Dinah were paired above.

The sexual power of artistic vocation is at once a source of pride
and uneasiness for Victorian feminist and protofeminist writers.
Because vocation, unlike other forms of work, was not immediately
or necessarily justifiable in terms of family, because the artist often

felt a need that went beyond earning a few pennies to support an ailing mother or an unemployed husband, the call to artistic endeavor was often perceived as a call away from family. Elizabeth Gaskell expressed this fear to an aspiring female writer when she claimed she could not have written novels when her children were younger because her "fictitious people" would have interrupted her dealings with the "real people" that called for her almost constant attention.[4] Stepping out of the family was, of course, seen as a step into the sexual wilderness.

The apparent contradiction between vocation and family was rhetorically resolved in a number of different ways. An 1853 article on women writers that appeared in the *North British Review* cautioned married women to take up fiction writing only if they could attend first to other, more important jobs, such as child-rearing. In an important logical inversion, however, the article goes on to maintain that *only* married women should write novels:

> If the novel addresses itself to the heart, what more natural than that it should then reach it most usefully and perfectly when coming from the heart of a woman ripe with all the dignity of her sex, full of all wifely and motherly experience?[5]

Although the author of the article admires certain novels by single women, notably *Uncle Tom's Cabin* and *Jane Eyre*, he feels even they lack the "full, and wholesome and most womanly perfection" of *Mary Barton*; even *Jane Eyre* is "unwomanly" while *Villette* is a veritable betrayal of femininity. A young lady novelist is, according to the article, "perpetually swaying between these three dangers: of being abstract, or morbid, or something like—we must mention the word immodest" (*North British Review*, p. 91).

In the rhetoric of this piece, novel writing grows out of maternal and domestic duties. By placing writing on a natural continuum with appropriately domestic notions of womanhood, the logic of the article allows it a cultural space within the household. Women who began to capitalize on the potentially liberating aspects of this formulation wanted to escape the constrictions of the female role without leaving the safety of home and domesticity. Writers on women's vocation used a series of domestic and maternal metaphors to legitimize their own and other women's struggles to express their creativity.

The domestication of the vocational impulse, however, is in its own coded way as much an expression of sexuality as a denial of it. It is the harnessing of sexual and physical energy into channels traditionally deemed appropriate for women. In a culture where housework was one of the few sanctioned physical activities even marginally available to women of the upper classes, and motherhood was the only appropriate expression of sexuality, domestic and maternal metaphors are coded expressions of various forms of female energy. Writers like Dinah Mulock Craik, Catherine Maria Sedgewick, Mrs. Humphrey Ward, and Elizabeth Gaskell went out of their way to domesticate their art, often constructing domestic narratives to justify or explain their own literary careers. Sedgewick, for example, claimed that her books were never the source of joy to her that her familial relations were, and went so far as to state that her cooking was the only accomplishment of which she was proud.[6] Gaskell explained her initial entrance into the field of fiction writing in terms of a family narrative; it is a Victorian commonplace that she began to write to console herself for the death of her son. Both Gaskell and Charlotte Tonna use the same domestic image to justify their taking to the pen; Tonna thanks her father for his encouragement, "without which my little talent might have laid by in a napkin all my days," while Gaskell defends Charlotte Bronte's vocation in the same idiom: "She must not hide her gift in a napkin; it was meant for the use and service of others."[7]

Gaskell's advice to the female writer was predictably couched in the most domestic terms; a letter to an aspiring author reads not so much like a treatise on writing as a guide to housework:

> I hope (for instance) you soap and soak your dirty clothes well before beginning to wash; and that you understand the comfort of preparing a dinner and putting it on to cook *slowly*, early in the morning, as well as having *always* some kind of sewing ready arranged to your hand, so you can take it up at any odd minute and do a few stitches.[8]

Dinah Mulock Craik talks in the same strain in her qualified defense of writing as a vocation for *some* women:

> The days of the blue-stockings are over. It is a notable fact that the best housekeeper, the neatest needlewomen . . . are ladies

[whose names] the world cons over in library lists and exhibition catalogues. I would give them now—except that the world has no possible business with them, except to read their books and look at their pictures.[9]

The ultimate collapsing of the literary into the domestic occurs with the first generation of British and American writers to produce both fiction and etiquette books. Craik, Tonna, Sedgewick, and Marian Harland, to name a few, all cross and combine genres frequently. Sedgewick's *Home*, to name one example, is both a short novel and an exemplary tale about household management, focussing as it does on a family run by Sedgewick's own principles of education and marriage.

The domestic metaphors that characterize these discussions of vocation do not immediately seem sexual or subversive. There is, however, a component of physicality in housework that Victorian protofeminists consistently used to their advantage. Harland and others describe housework as one of the few physical releases for the average middle-class woman; Harland contrasts idle, weak young ladies with busy housekeepers who take advantage of this "wholesome exercise of mind and body."[10] Her lamentations over mothers who protect their daughters from housework are appropriately expressed in physical terms:

> We [mothers] are cowardly, false to ourselves that we do not put it in practice—false to our trust, and cruel to our darlings in hardening our hands and muscles in order to keep theirs soft and flaccid   (Harland, p. 326).

Harland's ideal of the well-muscled housekeeper is antithetical to the aristocratic ideal of young ladyhood.

Domesticity also allows for the representation and reproduction of the female body in a number of interesting ways. While, as we have seen, etiquette books provided a space for the introduction of women's hunger, they also defined a territory in which women could talk specifically about the body in other ways. Numerous conduct books begin with the assertion that they are breaking the silence and taboo surrounding young women's physical self-knowledge. Many of these texts are self-consciously framed as revolutions in language. Within the confines of the subgenre, language tended to be extremely physical; etiquette book writers tended to see the moral world through the body. As one author put it when discussing the issue of childhood discipline: "evil enters into (a baby's) soul as the imperceptible atmosphere he breathes into his lungs." More graphically, Marian Harland concluded that young girls' diaries are "a pus channel by which morbid and gangrenous humors may be drained away." Women who crossed genres to write novels and conduct books used the latter and its conventions to take forbidden authority over the female body and the language used to describe it. The introduction of the domestic into the novel by even those writers that Elaine Showalter has labelled "conservative" can even be seen as a tentative step into the "wild zone" of truly physical women's language discussed in the final chapter of this study.[11]

Even more potentially subversive than domestic metaphors and equally coded, are discussions of vocation in terms of maternal images. Like the Biblical trope of the burning bush, the sentimentalized trope of motherhood is a seeming evasion of sexuality; and like the burning bush, "mother" introduces the female body at the point of its banishment. Connected with defensive domestic images, motherhood would seem to be cleansed of its sexual associations; instead it simultaneously sexualizes and sanctifies women's vocation. Craik plays on both the seeming invisibility and the sexuality of motherhood by comparing artistic vocation to the only completely sanctioned function of the female body:

> We may paint scores of pictures, write shelves full of books—the errant children of our brain may be familiar over half the known world, and yet we ourselves sit quietly by the chimney corner
>
> (Craik, p. 58).

Craik's use of the maternal metaphor provides a safe, even womb-like space for the limited expression of female sexuality. The invisibility of the mother's body in its displaced concern for its children becomes a sort of transparency through which one may read a highly sexual code.

Motherhood can, paradoxically, become a way of justifying leaving home and the domestic symbols which accrue around it. An 1876 editorial in *The Englishwoman's Review* explains:

> "An ounce of mother is worth a pound of clergy," says an old Spanish proverb, and we would add without derogation to orga-

nized civilization, it is worth a hundred-weight of Boards, Committees and Police. Our English economy teems with elaborately arranged systems, but they want the vitalizing warmth of women's work, and still more, of women's control—the *mother* influence and the benefit that would accrue to society by their more general *adoption* of public duties (second italics mine).[12]

The rhetoric of motherhood failed to salvage only one sort of female artist—the actress. Predictably, Craik couches the difference between the *artiste* and other "public women" in highly physical terms. She warns: [the actress] . . . needs to be constantly before the public, not only mentally but physically. The general eye becomes familiar not only with her genius but with her corporeality" (Craik, p. 58). The actress *as* body is a familiar trope in Victorian England; in *Mansfield Park* the young people betray inappropriate sexual feelings when they turn the house into an amateur theatre, Rochester trod "the old track . . . to shame and destruction" by taking an actress as his mistress, and Gwendolyn Harleth wants to become an actress at least partially to gratify her physical vanity. Actresses also displayed their corporeality in paintings; books about actresses tended to be highly illustrated and physically descriptive, while actresses frequently worked as painters' models. Ellen Terry herself announced her physicality to the Victorian world by proudly becoming a model for her first husband's paintings. Magdalen, in Wilkie Collins' *No Name*, makes her body public by deserting her sister for the stage; her punishment is constant physical scrutiny by the rest of the characters who pierce through her various costumes and disguises to distinguish a tell-tale mark on her neck. Walter, the narrator-hero of *My Secret Life*, sums up Victorian attitudes with a series of displacements; he reaches a turning point in his sexual knowledge when he has "learnt enough . . . to know that among men of his class the term lacemaker, along with actress and seamstress, was virtually synonymous with prostitute."[13]

It is Florence Nightingale who suggests a couternarrative of the actress. Although Craik halfheartedly domesticates artists "capering with set rouged smiles and leaden hearts" as well as "coarse screaming concert-singers" and "flaunting actresses" if they work "for the sake of the old parents, or the fiddler-husband and the sickly babies back home" (Craik, p. 61), Nightingale posits a new vision of the actress, built on a different idiom. In *Cassandra* she maintains that actresses are the only women whose work and privilege it is to study a text repeatedly and closely. The scholar-actress is no domestication; Nightingale is justifying one questionable career for women in terms of another.

Perhaps because of the vexed connection between genius and sexuality for women, few Victorian fictional heroines can be described as having a vocation. Those who do, notably in *Daniel Deronda* and *Aurora Leigh*, explore the empowering and limiting trope of motherhood. *Aurora Leigh* uses motherhood as an enabling archetype, only to abandon its erotic and revolutionary possibilities, while *Daniel Deronda* inverts the trope to produce a vision of vocation as a grotesque parody of motherhood. Both make explicit the connection between motherhood and eroticism hinted at in cultural documents of the period, and both alternate between the depiction of motherhood and its erasure.

Aurora Leigh has been seen by feminists such as Cora Kaplan as the ultimate Victorian attempt to inscribe the female body; Aurora's motto, taken from a painter friend, "paint the body well, you paint a soul by implication,"[14] would seem to privilege the physical as a ground for the generation of all art. In addition, the topography of the epic is anatomical; the body in general and the female body in particular are used throughout as a metaphor for writing: a poem has "tumors / warts and veins . . . implying life" (Bk. III, lines 42–43), money earned by writing popular articles gives "breathing-room / for body and verse" (Bk. III, lines 322–28). Images of childbirth, breastfeeding, and menstruation converge with images of female work to provide a gynocentric grid for Browning's poetics. Book V of the poem is traditionally seen as an invocation of the female body:

> Aurora Leigh be humble. Shall I hope
> To speak my poems in mysterious tune . . .
> With the human heart's large seasons, when it hopes
> And fears, joys, grieves and loves?—with all that strain
> Of sexual passion, which devours the flesh
> In a sacrament of souls? With mother's breasts
> Which, round the new-made creatures hanging there,
> Throb luminous and harmonious like pure spheres?
> (Bk. V, lines 1–18).

In this complex rendering of sexual paradox where "sex devours the flesh" to produce something spiritual, the poet sexualizes the maternal image only to reinscribe it as spiritual two lines later. The connection between motherhood and sexuality, often sentimentalized out of existence by Victorian mother-worship, is not only made explicit in the conjunction between "mother's breasts" and "sexual passion," but becomes part of the network of gynocentric images that constitute the poem.

The maternal body is, however, only glimpsed in this opening invocation. As mother's breasts are transfigured into "pure spheres," the genderless poet of the spheres replaces the voice of female experience. With the reference to the spheres, the female body is abstracted from the text. Taken in conjunction with other such abstractions, the mother's breasts become part of a submerged network of female images and the poem a palimpsest of female experience. Images of breasts and childbirth leave traces and scars, of course; various levels of the palimpsest are accessible to the reader. But, just as Aurora Leigh escapes the confinement of her aunt's house feeling "an escape of soul from body" (Bk. I, line 694), so the poem escapes the physical in its desire for genderless transcendence, the sacrament of souls over the gratification of the body. "Paint the body well / you paint the soul by implication" acquires a new teleology; the body, it seems, is merely a stopping-point on the journey to the soul. As the mother image appears and disappears, the text simultaneously sexualizes and abstracts vocation.

Equally complex and equally contradictory are the uses of the mother metaphor in *Daniel Deronda* where the actress Alcharisi explicitly chooses her vocation over motherhood by deciding to give Daniel away while she pursues her acting career. Interestingly, acting itself becomes a form of pregnancy; she explains: "I was living myriad lives in one. I did not want a child."[15] In giving birth to a variety of selves instead of a child, Alcharisi is, in terms of the text, enacting a solipsistic and parodic inversion of motherhood. She is aptly punished by a disease which too seems to be a replacement for a child: "A fatal illness has been growing inside me for a year" (Eliot, Bk. VII, p. 25). The child then is displaced, first by vocation and then by a tumor. Alcharisi's gothic use of the maternal metaphor invokes similar images in Mary Shelley's *Franken-*

stein where both childbirth and the quest for knowledge take on the sinister shape of transgression against nature.

Alcharisi explicitly identifies herself as part of Shelley's tainted matriarchal line by invoking monsterhood. In her description of what it means to be a Jewish woman she concludes: "Every woman is supposed to have the same set of desires, or else to be a monster" (Eliot, p. 691). Alcharisi's transgressions are both sexual and rhetorical; in her use of the maternal metaphor for vocation she explores its most subversive implications. The nurturant spiritualized mother becomes the sexual rebel who controls her own body until retribution overtakes it. The cautious strategic use of the maternal metaphor by writers like Gaskell, Josephine Butler, and Craik gives way to images of pain, disease, sexuality, and conflict which in turn converge to become part of the Gothic sub-text of the meticulously realistic *Daniel Deronda*.

Mothering and domesticity move from a possible to a necessary condition for the carrying out of vocation, to a structuring metaphor for vocation itself. The *North British Review*'s acceptance of married women authors becomes a stricture against "young lady writers" who should be "gently and with all reverence" told "to find for [their] gifts other employment" (p. 92). These in turn give way to a series of metaphors that unfold in increasingly sexual complexity.

The call to artistic endeavor is, then, a call to the female body to make an appearance in the interstices of Victorian texts and in the vehicles of metaphor. These appearances, short-lived and self-deconstructing as they are, leave their traces in nineteenth-century discussion of vocation. Vocation becomes a marked subject, the rhetoric that surrounds it rich with the possibility of female physicality. The bodies of the three Victorian heroines who at least temporarily answer the call, Dinah Morris, Aurora Leigh, and Alcharisi, come and go in a varied choreography of tropes, leaving in their wake a powerful sense of remembered physical and sexual presence.

The prostitute, the figure for other heroines' work, the unspeakable but ever-present example, has no such physical presence, either in the Victorian canon or in the culture at large. The prostitute's fundamental absence in an age obsessed by counting, categorizing, and rescuing her attests to the paradoxical nature of Victorian sexual sensibility. William Acton's "seminal" treatise on the subject reveals the blankness at the heart of so many Victorian conceptions of the prostitute when he explains "sexual desires of her own play but little part in inducing profligacy in the female."[16] Like Rossetti's Jenny, Acton's prostitute is a cipher of displaced lust; her body, indeed her very existence, is vicarious, her body and its urges invisible.

The language in which other Victorian observers and sexologists describe prostitutes underscores her sexual neutrality, her physical invisibility and—a related concept—her function as a symbol or figure rather than human being. She is "an object of lust," and "instrument of vice" and, finally, "the supreme type of vice" (Harrison, p. 244). In an otherwise graphic portrayal of a prostitute whose features were made unrecognizable by syphilis, William Arnot reveals her lack of body; "that imbruted soul and bloated body, with hardly any features left, a mass of horrible corruption now. That lump of living flesh was once a woman" (Harrison, p. 245). The features of many London prostitutes, erased and razed by syphilis, become an apt emblem of the prostitute's invisibility, a synecdoche for her strangely fleshless fleshiness. The "lump of flesh" at once foregrounds the body and reduces it to featurelessness, forces the reader to gaze on the horrible, and renders it invisible.

The erasure of the prostitute's body is only one way of creating bodily absence; another, perhaps more powerful way was not so much to get rid of the body as to dress it. The metaphor of dress is carried out on many levels; the reformers who addressed the problem of prostitution, the Victorian authors and painters who focussed more on the prostitute's clothing than on what it covered are all dressers of a sort. The final step in dressing the prostitute's body is its cloaking in conventional metaphor; in a culture where food and work were described in terms of sex, so was sex described in metaphors of food and work. Henry Mayhew's story of the veiled prostitute who haunted the parks of London becomes an allegory of this sort of dressing; according to Mayhew the veil lent an air of mystery to the prostitute; in effect, sexuality was projected onto the veil (p. 222). Writers of guidebooks to brothels provided metaphoric clothing of another sort. In carefully worded extended metaphors, men compared one prostitute or brothel with another:

> The abbess has just put the kipehook on all other purveyors of the French flesh market. She does not keep her meat too long on the hooks, though she will have her price; but nothing to get stale here. You may have your meat dressed to your own liking, and there is no need of cutting twice from one joint; and if it suits your taste, you may kill your own lamb or mutton.[17]

The elaborate euphemism of this extract from *The Man of Pleasure's Pocket Book* cloaks the body both for purposes of disguise and titillation. The reference to "meat dressed to your own liking" is part of a sexual continuum that uses as its medium dresses, disguise, costume, and self-conscious figuration.

Absence and dressing appear as sometimes overlapping alternatives to the depiction of the Victorian prostitute in art and literature. Absence seems to be the primary motif in fiction of the period; the Victorian novel is haunted by a series of dim, shadowy figures that hover on the margins of canonical texts. They are warnings in whispers, implied contrasts to heroines; like the governess, they hint at alternate tragic endings—they partake of none of the physicality which, in turn, haunts the Victorian canon. Helen in Alcott's *Work* and Martha in *David Copperfield* are figures that vanish into blankness at a touch. Martha moves in and out of the text like a spectre, a "flitting figure" who follows David through the storm leaving no footprints in the snow. Her body leaves no marks, no traces; she is already in a world beyond the body where she can serve only as a sign for other women not to follow in her curiously unmarked path. She identifies herself to Little Emily in terms of another world, as "a ghost that calls her from beside her open grave" (Dickens, p. 721). Helen is part of the same iconography; like Martha she flees to the river where she is represented as a dim, white figure, about to obliterate her own body by drowning. Alcott's feminism allows her and her heroine, Christie, to recuperate Helen from blankness and to take her from the water's edge to the city. Despite Christie's efforts, however, Helen can never again be accepted by the world in which she once worked. Helen disappears from Christie's life and from the text, to reemerge only when Christie herself enacts her own erasure in her attempted suicide on the banks of the same river.

Perhaps the best articulated and most vivid blankness is Carry Brattle's in Trollope's *Vicar of Bullhampton*. In a novel about the power to speak the difficult and the unspeakable, Trollope's treatment of the Carry Brattle subplot is a deliberate rendering of the nothingness that surrounds the Victorian prostitute. Trollope's hesitating preface sets the tone for a novel which might or might not have a place for the Carry Brattles of the world: "There arises, of course, the question of whether a novelist, who professes to write for the amusement of the young of both sexes, should allow himself to bring upon his stage a character such as that of Carry Brattle."[18] The preemptive apology is in itself an example of the representational paradox that forms the core of the novel; while Trollope in his preface and the narrator in the novel use Carry's full name at all times, her family and the other characters in the novel cannot name her until the end. Trollope's very apology, then, introduces Carry Brattle in her full identity; the question of whether Carry should be introduced at all is answered in Trollope's symbolic insistence on her full name.

Carry's entrance into the novel is announced by hesitation. The morphology of her introduction, the very syntax of the sentence that introduces without naming her, sets Carry off from the rest of the family into a seemingly unrecoverable silence. The sequence of siblings is seen through the eyes of Fanny, the "good" sister: "Between [Fanny's older brother] and Fanny there was—perhaps it would be better to say there had been—another daughter" (Trollope, p. 33). Predicate and punctuation combine to distance the reader from Carry's existence. Carry is elsewhere defined in terms of absence for her family: Fanny wanders desolate through her bedroom thinking of the series of sisters who no longer sleep there. One is married, and one dead; Carry's absence is made vivid by the lack of conventional explanation for her absence. Carry's lack of bodily presence in the novel is perhaps most clearly articulated in her father's decree that her name should not be spoken; Fanny cannot even use the word "sister" without adding her married sister's last name for fear of contradicting her father's decree of silence.

The silence that envelops Carry's family is infectious. The Vicar of Bullhampton, whose status as the novel's hero seemingly depends on his ability to name the unnamable, struggles when it comes to naming Carry. The Vicar is the only character in the novel who can name women with freedom; he tells his wife "not to be a fool" on many occasions, and goes so far as to call Mary Lowther, the heroine of the novel, an "ass" for not being able to make up her mind about marriage. In a dialogue that encapsulates the difficulty of naming women, the Vicar tries to persuade the Marquis of Trowbridge of the necessity of reclaiming Carry by referring to the Marquis' own daughters. The ensuing confrontation, "My daughters!" "Yes, your daughters, my Lord." "How dare you mention my daughters," attests to the silence in which women's lives are meant to be shrouded (Trollope, p. 112). By breaking through this silence, the Vicar is preparing to confront Carry's corporeal reality; soon after this confrontation with the Marquis, which almost causes him to be defrocked, the Vicar goes in search of Carry herself.

The actual moment of physical discovery is a miracle of euphemism and displacement. Carry's body is not mentioned; in the long description of her face and home, words associated with prostitutes come up only twice: Her curls are described as "more tawdry than of yore," and we are told Carry has a "disreputable looking novel in her hand" (p. 156). Carry's sexuality is synecdochally displaced onto her hair and her book, and into the long literary tradition that identifies women as texts and in terms of their hair. Milton's Eve's "wanton ringlets" foreshadow her fall; Jenny, Hester Prynne, and a long series of other heroines are texts written in an unfamiliar language.

Synecdoche and displacement also mark the Vicar's request that Carry come home. In a metonymic rendition of her body he instructs her, "Keep your hands clean. You know what I mean, and I will find some spot for your weary feet" (p. 161). Carry's body enters the text in fragments; hands, feet, and curls, acceptable parts of the body, stand cleanly for the unnamable whole. The Vicar's "you know what I mean" is an implicit admission of the codedness of his request of the more complete body that stands behind his words and of the fragmentation of the female body language and convention force upon him.

Carry's entrance into the text is by necessity fragmentary and painful. Monique Wittig and other feminist theorists suggest that such entries for women into textuality and into language are always painful in that they always involve a shattering of the silence which enshrouds women's physical presence. Carry's hands and feet are only a foreshadowing of Wittig's broken j/e in which she represents the pain of the female "I"'s entrance into representation.[19]

It is a long way from Carry's first entry to her final and limited acceptance. A major step toward her representation seems to be Mrs. Fenwick's the Vicar's wife, carefully embedded mention of Carry's physicality. Unlike her husband, Mrs. Fenwick has always feared naming the unpleasant; when the Vicar hypothetically mentions the possibility of her running away from him, she begs him not to mention such a terrible subject. Mrs. Fenwick hesitates to name Carry and in her hesitation comes by accident upon her body. In explaining that she has trouble dealing with prostitutes as individual cases, she says "there are so many . . . and I do not know how they are to be treated except in a body" (Trollope, p. 251). This notion of body is, of course, as constricting as it is liberating; it is, indeed, an erasure rather than a recognition of individual presence. The introduction of the word, however, has a power of its own that is neither completely predictable nor completely in accordance with its origin. Mrs. Fenwick's slip that introduces the body in the act of its denial prepares the way for and is analagous to the Vicar's plan of reintroducing Carry physically into her family.

The plan is, of course, more than a stratagem. The physical introduction of Carry is consistent with the whole structure of the novel which has been, throughout, obsessed with the problem of bodily representation. Carry's physical presence in her father's house is an unpredictable and perhaps dangerous shattering of the code of silence. Like Mrs. Fenwick's mention of the word "body," it can have almost any consequence, but, as a gesture, seems to have a persuasive power almost entirely cut off from its original meaning.

When Carry does enter the house, a further displacement takes place. In a novel which, even for Trollope, is startlingly devoid of sexual passion, Carry's sexuality is projected onto her mother's embrace. Her mother covers her with the "warm, thick, clinging kisses, not with reassurance" (Trollope, p. 343) that have been missing from both the Carry Brattle subplot and Mary Lowther's tentative courtships.

The novel ends in mitigated happiness for all parties and, not surprisingly, in mitigated representation for Carry. After a month of living with his daughter, Sam Brattle refers to her by her first name. Carry is far from oblivious of the significance of this act; she has, in fact, told her sister she will run away again if her father does not come to use her name. The final naming of Carry Brattle becomes an acceptance for Sam and the reader of her physical presence and an admission in and into the language of her body.

The Vicar of Bullhampton is remarkable among Victorian novels for its foregrounding of the relation of sexuality to representation. In a slightly different way, other Victorian texts and paintings enact this relation by metaphoric dressing of the prostitute's body.[20] The act of dressing the body, epitomized in the apocryphal anecdote in which they covered even piano legs in demure little "skirts," becomes an important cultural statement. As the century progressed, "dresses" of all kinds became more elaborate; the Victorian novelists, the aesthetes, and the Pre-Raphaelites rejoiced in lavish extended metaphor in their novels, poems, and paintings, often allowing women's dresses a life of their own.

The descriptions of Nancy and the other prostitutes in *Oliver Twist* focus far more obsessively on what they put on than on what they take off; Oliver's first observations, that they have "a good deal of hair" and "a great deal of colour in their faces," emphasize dress and artificiality over nudity and sensuality. Nancy's costumes proliferate as the novel progresses. With the aid of curlers and an apron from Fagin's "inexhaustible stock" of disguises, she pretends to be Oliver's sister. Toward the middle of the novel, as she begins to sympathize with Oliver, she spies on Sykes and Fagin, covering herself with a shawl to make herself invisible. Slipping into the novel's dark corners, head and body swathed in her shawl, she becomes a symbol of self-erasure and vicariousness. Her murder is a final dressing, a revelation of her as typological:

> It was a ghastly figure to look upon. The murderer, staggering backward to the wall and shutting out the sight with his hand, seized a heavy club and struck her down.[21]

Nancy, neutralized into an "it," a "figure," is easy prey. Her last act, the holding up of Rose's handkerchief to Heaven, is a final covering, a gesture that makes metaphorically possible Sykes' denial of her corporeality as he covers his eyes. The reader too sees not Nancy, but the death of a symbol whose function is simultaneously the representation of illicit sexuality and the denial of the body.

The covering of the prostitute's body is reiterated in Victorian paintings of women. Perhaps the most famous painting of a prostitute is Rossetti's obsessively revised *Found*. The woman in the picture shrinks away from its center, her body covered in layers of shawls, her face partially shrouded by an oversized bonnet. The folds of the shawls and the bonnet catch the light and reflect it back, concealing the body beneath. Like Nancy, the woman in *Found* muffles her body until her clothes come to stand for herself.

In a series of paintings not precisely of prostitutes but of fallen women, clothing, its patterns and its textures, dominates and at times erases the bodies beneath it. William Morris' *Queen Guinevere*, Rossetti's *Persephone*, William Holman Hunt's *The Awakening Conscience*, and Frank Cadogan Cowper's *La Belle Dame Sans Merci* are all, in some sense, renditions of fabric. The pattern of Guinevere's dress provides a motif for the rest of the painting and is echoed in the wallpaper and curtains. The dark folds of Persephone's gown obscure her body from view; her hair and her dress meet darkly to make the painting almost unfathomable. The bright detail of the woman's scarf in *The Awakening Conscience* distracts the eye from the curves of her body, while the flaming red and gold of the dress of *La Belle Dame Sans Merci* draws the viewer's eye to the texture of the fabric and away from the woman herself. Indeed, in this painting which might be read as Pre-Raphaelitism's last gasp, the dress seems sinisterly to stand alone above the body of the dead knight.

Pre-Raphaelite dresses, with their power to dwarf the female body, become aligned with the paintings' typically ornate frames: become, in a sense, framing devices themselves. Delores Rosenblum and others have discussed the sinister implications of modelling for the Pre-Raphaelites; for her and for others, Christina Rossetti, Elizabeth Siddal, and the series of women obsessively and endlessly painted by members of the Brotherhood, are "killed into art." While not all of them sacrificed their bodies to their representation as literally as Siddal, who posed day after day in a full cold bathtub for *Ophelia*, modeling, as Christina Rossetti's poetry makes clear, is fraught with danger as well as excitement.[22]

The dresses that come to stand for fallen women stand also for Victorian projections from the prostitute's body onto external objects. The play of tropes that describe vocation takes the opposite journey; the use of the mother metaphor signals a turning inward, an exploration not only of the body but of its innermost recesses. In a sense, the trope of motherhood is, for the Victorians, antimetaphoric: The metatrope that seems to govern discussion of the figurative language is precisely the trope of "home"; metaphors are typically seen as journeys away from home, away from the security of "original" meaning.[23] Tonna's suspicion of metaphor discussed in Chapter II translates itself easily, in Victorian rhetorical logic, into the consistent employment of maternal and domestic metaphors. The Victorian preoccupation with realism, and Victorian women's preoccupation with domestic realism, provide another layer of cover for the richness of metaphor. The flamboyant metaphoric "dressing" of the prostitute is, of course, the opposite form of cover, where the covering fabric itself becomes the entire text.

It is not the place of this study to determine which rhetorical alternative, which trope, "mother" or "dress," is more "realistic," "representative," or even fully sexualized. It is in the movement of these tropes, in the constant shifting between representation and cover-up *within* the structuring metaphors, that female sexuality makes its presence felt. It is in the traces that record the paths of such movement that we come to a fleeting and always incomplete vision of the female body. In this choreography of tropes, nothing "stands" for anything else; one trope simply records the movements and possibilities of another.

CHAPTER IV

Body, Figure, Embodiment:
The Paradoxes
of Heroine Description

In the sixth chapter of *The Small House at Allington,* Anthony Trollope gives a delayed description of his sister-heroines, the "two pearls of Allington," Lily and Bell Dale. He opens the chapter with an admission that he has so far been remiss in avoiding a physical description of the two girls:

> I am well aware that I have not as yet given any description of Bell and Lilian Dale, and equally well aware that the longer the doing so is postponed the greater the difficulty becomes. I wish it could be understood without any description that they were two pretty, fair-haired girls, of whom Bell was the tallest and prettiest, whereas Lily was almost as pretty as her sister, and perhaps was more attractive.[1]

The narrator's disingenuous "wish" that this two-line description will suffice is belied by the meticulously chronicled description of Lily and her sister that takes up the next two pages. Trollope's extended description is full of details, emendations, and scrupulous qualifications: "Lily was the shorter of the two, but the difference was hardly remembered unless the two were together." "The two girls were very fair, so that the soft tint of color which relieved the whiteness of their complexion was rather acknowledged than distinctly seen. It was there, telling its own tale of health, as its absence would have told a tale of present or coming sickness; and yet nobody could ever talk about the colour in their cheeks." "It was

79

C. Grant, illustration for Trollope's *The Small House at Allington*.
(New York: 1905), photograph by Allan Kobernick.

not flaxen hair, and yet it was very light. Nor did it approach auburn; and yet there ran through it a golden tint that gave it a distinct brightness of its own." "Bell's teeth were far more even than her sister's; but then she showed her teeth more frequently" (*Small House*, pp. 71–72).

Despite its careful framing as an evenhanded comparison between the two sisters, this proliferation of detail graphically betrays what the narrator has admitted to in an earlier chapter—his love for and fascination with Lily Dale (*Small House*, p. 18). Lily's "attractiveness," which, opposed throughout the novel to her sister's "prettiness," is the source of both her downfall and her interest as a character, excites the narrator into representational excess. Her description is a litany of parts; her lips, eyes, chin, dimples, hair, and teeth are placed on view for the reader who is invited to enter into the narrator's obsession. Despite the meticulousness of the detail and the narrative entry into the mouth where Lily so carefully guards the secret of her teeth, Lily's body is oddly absent from this description. Her sensuality is expressed through a series of Victorian codes, among them physiognomy and synecdoche, which will be discussed later in this chapter. The gaps in Trollope's description of Lily are both omissions and entrances, sites of repression and of fantasy.

In 1901, some fifty years after the publication of *Small House*, William Dean Howells spanned history and an ocean to insert himself at these sites of fantasy and between the lines of Trollope's description. Howells' *Heroines of Fiction* is frequently a penetration into the interstices of eighteenth- and nineteenth-century heroine description; bemoaning the sparseness of early descriptions, he participates vicariously in their fleshing out. His elaboration of Lily Dale swells an already extended description:

> If any reader happens himself to be of that period of the early eighteen-sixties to which Lily Dale's romantic young girlhood belonged—he will see her as she first appeared to Adolphus Crosbie. He will know that she wore a large hoop, which tilted enough when she played croquet to give a glimpse of her white stockings; that her loose sleeves were confined at the wrists with narrow linen cuffs matching a little linen collar at her neck; and that everything was very plain and smooth about her. She would have on a pork-pie hat . . .[2]

Howells' belated participation in the description of Lily Dale is noteworthy for several reasons. Perhaps most obvious upon reading this passage is Howells' sense of shared fantasy, nostalgic, voyeuristic, and sexual, predominantly, perhaps entirely, male. The revealing shift from a description of her clothing to what the clothing in turn reveals, taken in conjunction with the male pronoun which announces this journey back in literary time, marks Lily's physical description as a sexual issue and Howells' intrusion as a sexual act. His appeal to other readers who share with him his vision of the eighteen-sixties and their embodiment in this female form places the act of description in a context that moves beyond idiosyncrasy to a communal, and therefore a political, context.

Also crucial in reading Howells' description of Lily is an understanding of the impulse that motivated his supplementation of Trollope's already meticulous description. The impulse is a central one in an analysis of Victorian culture and in the phenomenon of realism itself. In his description, Howells is addressing himself both to the inherent limitations of realism—its inability to tell one everything one wants to know—and to the taboos that governed both the perception and representation of women's bodies in the Victorian era and beyond. As we shall see later, Trollope's description of Lily is governed by a series of representational taboos— rhetorical codes that conceal in the very act of depiction. Howells' supplementary description is an attempt to move beyond these limitations to lift the veil of Victorianism for the viewing pleasure of the early twentieth-century reader. In simultaneously traveling back to the eighteen-sixties and wrenching Lily from her Victorian context, Howells promises to free Lily from the prudery of his own insertion into the text.

Perhaps predictably, this act of rescue inscribes itself within the very conventions it tries to transcend. It is no accident that Howells' description of Lily should focus so obsessively on her clothing, on the very signs of Victorianism, the very emblems of its prudery. If Howells removes Lily's hoop skirt even for the time it takes her to take a shot in croquet, it is only, paradoxically to reveal her foot, clothed in virginally white stockings and in itself, as we have seen in earlier chapters, a typically Victorian synecdoche for the unnameable parts of Lily's body.

Perched as she is in the ever-shifting center of the series of paradoxes that frame the depiction of women's bodies and Victorian representation in general, Lily's body and its entrances into textuality and sexuality are prime candidates for the sexual/rhetorical act of intrusion, unveiling, and reveiling. Sensual but still unequivocally a "good girl," refusing to be "missish or coy" about her love, but preserving "a dignity of demeanour" throughout, described in loving detail yet strangely unrepresented, Lily epitomizes both the bodilessness and the sensuality of the Victorian fictional heroine. Lily reappears throughout this chapter, alternately "captured" by representational codes and breaking through them with the strength of her own physicality.

The impulse to flesh out skeletal descriptions is not only a naturalist response to Victorianism, but part of a historical continuum, a process of revision and rewriting in which the Victorians occupied a vexed and interesting position.[3] Mary Cowden Clarke's *The Girlhood of Shakespeare's Heroines* does for Shakespeare what *Heroines of Fiction* does for Trollope and other nineteenth-century novelists. Operating in the representational fissures of Shakespeare's plays, Clarke provides a series of his most famous heroines with an ancestry, a girlhood, and a detailed physical description. Lady Macbeth is, perhaps surprisingly, blonde, with "locks like golden beams of morning . . . eyes the colour of an azure lake when it reflects the serene expanse of a summer day."[4] Clarke draws Lady Macbeth even further into Victorian conventions of representation by providing a long physiognomist's reading of her face:

> Surpassingly handsome she was; but yet a look was there in those blue eyes, that marred their loveliness of shape and colour and seemed sinisterly to contradict their attractive power. In the mouth too, around those full and rubied lips, and amid those exquisite dimples, there played certain lines that presented indications of a startling contrast of will and unfeminine flexibility with so much charm of feature, which might have produced sensations of repulsive surmise to one accustomed to seek charm in expression rather than in linear beauty   (Clarke, p. 110).

The sentimentality of this description cannot disguise Clarke's desire to provide Lady Macbeth with a body and to account in some way for her physicality. Clarke's translation of Lady Macbeth's physical power into the highly codified language of Victorian description is both an attempt to capture her subject in idiom and to free her from the limitations, chronological and generic, of the text in which she originally appears. Like Howells' discussion of Lily Dale, this attempt to provide Lady Macbeth with an existence outside the play is in itself as much an escape from the body as a recognition of it. Clarke's description, founded as it is on the important Victorian codes of physiognomy or moralized description and cliché, distances both author and reader from the female body that is its subject.

Physiognomy and cliché are not, of course, the only two linguistic codes that create a gap between the reader and the Victorian heroine's body, or, for that matter, from any represented object. These codes are, in all probability, innumerable, and are a necessary component of all language. Linguists from Augustine to Derrida have devoted much of their work to an analysis of the space between signifier and signified, between representation and the represented.[5] By focussing on the codes of cliché, synecdoche, and metatrope, and on the depiction of the heroine, this chapter explores the question of coding as it applies to the female body. Without suggesting that perfect representation is possible, it will center both on the use of distancing codes and on the power of these codes to subvert themselves. I suggest that the distance between the heroine's body and the words used to describe it are not simply *differance*, but an aggravated and deeply political instance of culture intervening between a subject and its representation.

This chapter locates its examination of Victorian representational codes in moments of heroine description, a term that includes, but is not limited to, the heroine's first appearance in the text. It centers on all moments of physical entry, all announcements of presence, all language about physical appearance, which, in the terms of this study, is frequently recast as physical disappearance.

Very little has been written on the problem of description in general, even less on character description, still less on the specific description of the female body.[6] Description has typically been dismissed "as a sort of figure's hyperbole, discourse ornaments' ornament, a sort of superlative process whose excess must be controlled carefully"[7] and description of a character's external appearance (prosopography) as valuable only in an ancillary relationship to moral description.[8] It also suffers from the "danger" that it might introduce into the text "foreign vocabularies," or specialized terms that in turn introduce the "trace of *work* into the literary text" (Hamon, p. 9). A description of a house, for example, would allow for the introduction of architectural terms, a description of a painting would involve a series of specialized terms like perspective, chiaroscuro, and so on. It would seem appropriate to suggest that physical description, through the introduction of the body, posits a connection between work (in this case biology) and sexuality. Because of the connection discussed earlier between work and sex, this makes physical description doubly sexual, doubly fragile, doubly taboo.

The act of description itself is heavily coded in physical terms. Hamon cites examples of description "which appear to us to be more or less foreign bodies; not assimilable; a sort of radically different textual cyst" (Hamon, p. 10). The casting of description as ornament suggests its seductiveness. As both cyst and ornament, description becomes a form of sexual disease, an eruption in the text that has a life and erotic energy of its own.

Heroine description would seem to be an important focal point in the Victorian novel. Because so many Victorian novels focus on the adventures of a physically beautiful heroine and consider for so many pages the disposition of her body in marriage or death, Victorian heroine description would seem to bear many of the burdens of realism; the novel must in effect conjure up the body which will claim our attention over hundreds of pages until it is properly disposed of. This burden, as Jeanne Fahnestock indicates, became heavier with the passage of the century; by the end of the Victorian era descriptions had become almost obsessive in their cataloguing of features; in Fahnestock's words, "minute detail replaced generalities . . . the heroine came out of the shadows and into focus" (Fahnestock, p. 326). These details themselves, however, bore the burden of both disclosure and concealment as each code in its different way contributed to a double and self-erasing portrait of the heroine.

Physiognomy or moralized description is perhaps the most widely discussed of Victorian representational codes. Fahnestock explains:

> [Writers] could achieve . . . the effects [of psychological description] . . . dramatically and concisely if they gave instead details of physical description which stood for character traits. Of course this description only worked if writers and readers shared a system of meaning, a code for translating descriptive terminology into aspects of personality   (Fahnestock, p. 325).

Fahnestock herself shares in this passage a teleology common to the Victorians; by emphasizing the "higher uses" to which physical description can be put, she is justifying physical description in terms of a larger enterprise. The heroine's body disappears to be immediately replaced by a more spiritualized account of her psyche. Fahnestock recognizes and identifies the code but, in effect, reads it only one way.

This chapter is particularly concerned with three less visible representational codes as they have been used to describe and conceal the female body. It examines the role of cliché or dead metaphor, synecdoche, and metatrope in shaping and confining the heroine's body. This list of codes is, of course, not exhaustive; the three codes detailed here are themselves synecdoches for the larger codedness of the body, metaphor, the novel and the realist project itself.

As we shall see, cliché or dead metaphor is only subjectively a separate category from metaphor which has itself been seen by feminists from Charlotte Tonna to Adrienne Rich as a rhetorical trick that distracts the reader from tenor to vehicle, from the "realities" of female bodily experience to a more seductive abstraction.[9] While the final chapter of this study looks at the power of metaphor to kill its subject, this chapter focusses on the accusation that some metaphors are themselves dead, killed by overuse, and the implications of this murder for the "bringing to life" of female characters. Itself a special instance of metaphor, briefly explored in the discussion of Carry Brattle and prostitution in Chapter III, synecdoche is both a way of introducing sexuality by implication and a fragmentation and fetishization of culturally selected parts of the female body. The hand or arm that comes to stand for the unnameable body parts at once introduces the larger body by implication and focusses the reader's attention on disembodied fragments.

The last section of the chapter concerns itself with what I will call the doubled metaphor or metatrope, where the figure used to describe a heroine is conventionally recognizable as itself a chain of metaphors, an elaborate sign system that must be carefully interpreted. Heroines throughout the nineteenth century in both Britain and America were constantly being compared to paintings, sculptures, books, or pieces of music. This metaphor which opens out into increasingly conscious figuration provides a double frame, two layers of code through which the heroine must be "read." The doubled hermeneutics required of readers distances them geometrically from the heroine's body; Dorothea Brooke's body recedes into the distance as it is framed first in language, then through a series of comparisons to paintings, and then by a debate over the relative representational powers of painting and writing. Other heroines are distanced from their lovers and their readers by appearing as either texts or as works (objects) of art.

Like the heroines they depict and entrap, all three codes have the simultaneous power of presence and absence, the ability to frame and to self-destruct. The example in Chapter II of Dinah's erasure and subsequent reinscription of the body with the use of the same distracting trope shows both the power and the weakness of the codes that dictate her safe physical journey into language. Individual authors, of course, use the codes with different effect; codedness itself makes pronouncements on what is conventional and what is subversive very difficult. My close but not, I hope, closed, readings of particular texts provide a context for determining whether a particular rhetorical figure is being used subversively or not. The correct identification of a particular figure as subversive or conventional, itself a problematic dichotomy in texts that depend for their richness on shifting and effervescent rhetorical play, is less important than the acknowledgment of the potential richness and physicality of Victorian literature and culture. The heroine's body can never, perhaps should never, be fully "captured" in language; it appears and disappears from the texts that are its stages in an intricate choreography of tropes,[10] a dance that itself bespeaks physicality.

My readings of novels in terms of codes is hardly original; my project differs essentially from Roland Barthes'[11] in the constant inclusion of mirror-readings where codes that have been read as constriction are reread and reenvisioned as liberating and vice versa. The mirror, with its infinite potential for multiplication and distortion, its opposite connotations of vanity and introspection, is a particularly apt figure for reflection of and upon the female body. Unlike Gilbert and Gubar, I do not see breaking through the mirror as the central feminist project; my readings take place on the surface of the mirror, in the scratches upon it carved by the clients in "Jenny," in its crazy and distorting reflections, and in the bodies of the heroines mirrors fail to represent in the moment of reflection.

Dead Metaphor

One has only to look at the metaphors that inform the study of metaphor itself to see how closely figuration is implicated in sexual politics. The structuring tropes through which one "reads" metaphor, dress, figure, and home set up a network of opposing sexual value for "journeys" from the literal. On the one hand, metaphor is literal language "cunningly garbed," seductively and exotically dressed.[12] A metaphor is a journey from the safe "home" of literal language, a wandering through dangerous rhetorical labyrinths, the tracing of a streetwalker's path.[13] On the other hand, in a contemporary feminist construction, metaphor is the unnecessary ornament of the naked body suggested in the discussion of prostitution in Chapter III, a distraction from the nakedness of literal experience. While both views oversimplify the possibility of exchange between tenor and vehicle, between the sexuality of dress and nakedness, there is no doubt that the rhetoric of metaphor inscribes itself as sexual play with possible unplayful consequences.

An unplayful consequence that maintains its complicity in sexual debate is what many philosophers of language have come to call dead metaphor or cliché. Thus, Donald Davidson is able to speak of "the corpse of a metaphor"—of killing metaphor through overuse (Davidson, p. 36). It only further complicates matters to be told that dead metaphor is a theoretically bankrupt category—

a dead issue, so to speak.[14] The series of dead metaphors that describe the Victorian heroine and the death of debate about cliché is, in fact, a double murder, which in turn gives rise to a number of murders in self-defense. The "killing of the angel in the house" which paradoxically has itself become a feminist cliché for the "killing" of clichés is both a murderous response to the issue of dead metaphor and its silencing, and a potential theoretical suicide.[15] Once again, the theoretical movement necessary for understanding the political use of language is to refuse to break down distinctions that the "correct" use of literary theory commands us to do. It is the use of those very distinctions that has imprisoned women's bodies; to ignore them is to ignore real consequences of false dichotomies.

For the purpose of this section, there are in fact "dead" and "living" metaphors. They exist, of course, only as strategies in a representational murder. They are the alibis both Victorian and contemporary culture have come to believe. The operation of cliché in Victorian heroine description has several important consequences. First, it defines and perpetuates an unceasingly iterable notion of "woman"; all women are alike, all replaceable. Second, by reducing women's bodies to clichés, we deny the concept of individual or non-normative bodily experience and purge the deviant woman from representability. Third, cliché restricts sexual and intellectual arousal, making more possible a limited degree of enjoyment but erasing the potential for adventure. In the same way that repeated exposure to pornography both encourages and delimits sexual responses, the endless repetitions of cliché define an appropriate territory for engagement with the heroine's body. The lack of surprise involved in "dead" heroine descriptions underscores the heroine's role as subject and provides a linguistic frame beyond which she cannot stray.

We have already seen the imprisoning effect of cliché on Rossetti's Jenny, and how the poem begins the journey from her body by the use of conventional comparisons. For the purposes of figuration Jenny's sleep is a metaphorical death,[16] her absorption into an economy of signifiers as fatal to her body as it is to her monetary interests. The murder of Jenny begins with her momentary association with the angel that feminists must kill in self-defense; her eyes "like blue skies" and her hair like "countless gold" align Jenny with a series of women whom she emphatically is not. The particular comparison with the speaker's cousin Nell, who is also "fond of fun," is, on the one hand, liberating to Jenny; to some extent it makes her desires normative. Rhetorically, however, the introduction of Nell and her series of conventional attributes silences Jenny's differences and reproduces this silencing as physical.

The angel herself and the bodiless body of comparisons she evokes actually come to "personify" a series of Victorian heroines. At once a metaphor for femininity and for cliché, the angel becomes a ghost that haunts Victorian representation of women. Mary Cowden Clarke's incarnation/incarceration of Lady Macbeth attempts her transformation from murderess to the angel who must herself be murdered in language, strangled by cliché. Both Jenny and Clarke's Lady Macbeth are victims of a series of representational murders in which the authors are both necessarily and only partially complicitous. In widely different ways, both Rossetti and Clarke want to liberate the body; both, in effect, have to murder their own creation to do so.

The connection between the angel and the murder of the body through the murder of metaphor is carefully set out in what is, perhaps, the first "Victorian" novel, Mary Shelley's *Frankenstein*. Elizabeth, perhaps more than any other nineteenth-century heroine, *is* the angel in the house; she is also as much a construction of conventional tropes as the monster is a construction of conventional dead bodily parts. Like the monster's, Elizabeth's component parts are dead:

> Her hair was the brightest living gold, and, despite the poverty of her clothing, seemed to set a crown of distinction on her head. Her brow was clear and ample, her blue eyes cloudless, and her lips and the molding of her face so expressive of sensibility and sweetness that none could behold her without looking on her as of a distinct species, as being heaven-sent, and bearing a celestial stamp in all her features.[17]

While Frankenstein has been seen by Moers, Knoepflmacher, and others as an early inscription of the female body, the novel's physicality is inaccessible, buried within the bones and organs of the charnel house. Elizabeth's body provides a safe rhetorical surface upon which the conventional love story of the novel is written. It is dead from the beginning; ironically living female sexuality must be found somewhere else, in the novel's many underground searches and displacements. Elizabeth's murder on her wedding night is merely the fulfillment of necrophiliac writing and necrophiliac sexual desire. From the beginning of the novel, eroticism is associated with the death of language and with more "literal" death; both are linked with the transcription of the secrets of the female body.

In *Lady Audley's Secret*, Lucy/Helen's impersonation of an angel, the shrouding of her body in dead metaphor, makes her both a murderess and a suicide. Helen's angelic looks are instrumental in her transformation into Lucy and then into Lady Audley; she captivates wherever she goes because she is "too beautiful for earth," her curls forming "a pure halo around her head."[18] These instruments of captivation themselves lead first to her need to capture and murder her ex-husband, to her capture *by* Robert, the novel's detective figure, and ultimately to her capturing in language. Her husband's only clue to his wife's identity is a curl cut off at her supposed deathbed—part of the halo that both does and does not represent her identity. It is a description of Helen in her husband's letter to his sister at the time of her marriage that leads Robert to the final recognition of Lady Audley's double identity:

> The letter written almost immediately after George's marriage, contained a full description of his wife—such a description as a man could only write within three weeks of a love match—a description in which every feature was minutely catalogued, every grace of form or beauty of expression fondly dwelt upon, every charm of manner lovingly depicted   (Braddon, p. 138).

Robert's instant recognition of Lady Audley in George's description of Helen depends on the conventionality of the tropes each of them uses to perceive and to describe the woman whose body is the focus of all writing and reading in the novel. The language of the letters, the language of love, is easily turned by circumstance into the language of capture; the clichés of beauty which Lady Audley herself is so eager to perpetrate, close in and capture her by the end of the novel. Lady Audley is herself quite conscious about the sinister power of cliché. In teasing Robert about George's lasting affection for his supposedly dead wife, she says:

> I did not think men were capable of such deep and lasting affections. I thought that one pretty face was as good as another pretty face to them; and that when number one with blue eyes and fair hair died, they had only to look out for number two, with dark eyes and black hair, by way of variety (Braddon, p. 57).

In speaking to the iterability of the female body, Lady Audley is aware of her own successive and successful reincarnations. She knows that it is male clichés of female beauty that allow her to be both captivating and captured. The evening that made her Lady Audley and propelled her into bigamy was an evening marked by dead—perhaps murderous—metaphor:

> [Sir Michael] could no more resist the tender fascination of those soft and melting blue eyes; the graceful beauty of that slender throat and drooping head, with its wealth of showering flaxen curls; the low music of that gentle voice . . . than he could resist his destiny   (Braddon, p. 10).

The metaphors Sir Michael silently employs in the reading of his future wife are, like the speaker's in "Jenny," part of an economy in which women are replaceable. The very perception of Lucy as exceptional is based on a series of observations realized in only the most conventional language. Like Jenny's, Lady Audley's hair is immediately translated into gold, a signal that Lucy, like Jenny, is a good to be possessed as much by metaphor as by marriage.

The angel of figuration enables Helen Talboys to kill herself and rise again as Lady Audley; ultimately, however, the price is real suicide. Lady Audley dies of grief in a mental asylum, killed, this time, not only figuratively but "bodily." Isabel Vane of *East Lynne* undergoes the same journey from falsified death (metaphorical suicide) to a "real" death at the end of the novel. Interestingly, she too enters the text through the conduit of her lover's point of view, as an angel. Mr. Carlyle cannot grant the apparition that is Isabel corporeality in his first vision of her. "Who—what was it?" he asks himself. She was "not like a human being . . . more like an angel."[19] And, indeed, this angel also is a figure for dead figuration. To the extent that Isabel is described, it is as a series of dead metaphors that replicate their murderous potential in Isabel's false death and her bodiless return as governess to her own children. Isabel's beauty, like Lady Audley's, enables her to leave her husband, in Isabel's case, with a lover who deserts her. Like Lady Audley, Isabel cannot afford to be recognized; unlike her she chooses to hide, not behind clichés of beauty, but behind a scarred face and the dis-figuring spectacles of Mme. Vine.

Dead figuration also figures the death of desire. Lily Dale, whose sensuality, as we have seen, defies angelic "prettiness" and angelic description, appears first in *Small House* as a series of spontaneous and playful metaphors. After her rejection by Crosbie, the metaphors with which Lily describes herself become stagnant, killing themselves through repetition. By the end of *Last Chronicle of Barset*, the second novel in which she appears, she has murdered her own desire through the repetition of a single metaphor for herself and her body. Lily is first introduced in *Small House* in a chapter entitled "The Two Pearls of Allington"; later she epithetizes herself as a butterfly, a dragon, and a tree. None of these metaphors is in itself as important as the process of figuration that helps to move Lily from eager and loving sexuality at the beginning of *Small House* to erotic stasis at the close of *Last Chronicle*.

Lily's willingness to speak of herself and others in highly figurative language is, early on, one of her attractions. One of the first times we hear her speak, she is apostrophizing Crosbie, her future lover, as an "Apollo"; after she and Crosbie become engaged, she confesses to having given him a nickname, and this becomes a part of their sexual language. Lily's initial faith in metaphor to convey both truth and affection is evident when she tells Crosbie that a month with him has turned her into a butterfly. Focussing on the most conventional use of the term, Crosbie warns her that she must not be a butterfly when she is married. Lily's answer is a serious attempt to explain the erotic and liberating possibilities of metaphor: "No, not in that sense. But I meant my real position in the world—that for which I would fain hope that I was created—opened to me only when I knew you and knew that you loved me." Crosbie's reduction of Lily's language to dead metaphor kills their love and almost kills Lily. When he deserts her to marry Lady Alexandrina, he and his future bride exchange jokes about "wood nymphs"; he has, by the time he proposes to Alexandrina, persuaded himself that Lily is not human, that her body and spirit can be summed up by conventional figures.

By the end of *Last Chronicle*, Lily's own use of metaphor has changed; she has killed metaphor as she kills her own desire. In her repetitive refusals of Johnny Eames she sticks to one formulaic rejection, comparing herself to a split and shattered tree. This final self-figuration, like the initials "O. M." (Old Maid) she writes in her journal, serves as a linguistic sign of the death of her desire. By the time Johnny promises to write Lily once a year in the same words, begging her to be his wife, the killing of language and eroticism is complete, and spontaneous expressions of love and desire have lost their place in the novel.

If the death of metaphor figures the death of play and desire, it can also be a symptom of a love that is dead and worthless from the beginning. In Elizabeth Gaskell's *Wives and Daughters*, Roger must choose between Molly and her more conventionally beautiful stepsister, Cynthia. In describing Cynthia to his brother, Osborne, Roger searches among a catalogue of conventional companions to find a simile for her eyes:

> Miss Kirkpatrick's eyes must always be perfection. . . . I often try to find something in nature to compare them to; they are not like violets—that blue in the eyes is too like physical weakness of sight; they are not like the sky—that colour has something of cruelty in it.[20]

Osborne cuts through the rhetoric of comparison by parodying the search for simile:

> Come, don't go on trying to match her eyes as if you were a draper and they are a bit of ribbon; say at once 'her eyes are lodestars,' and have done with it! I set up Molly's grey eyes and curling black lashes, long odds above the other young woman's; but, of course, it's all a matter of taste   (Gaskell, p. 371).

The repetition of tropes can distract the reader as well as the lover from the body and its experiences. Fahnestock and others

have labelled *Adam Bede* an "anti-physiognomist" novel, but have
not identified conventional tropes, deadened metaphors, as one
source of the numbing to reality produced in the reader when he
or she makes the mistake of reading a character according to
physiognomy. Adam and the Poysers make the mistake of reading Hetty as physiognomists; the reader has constantly and ironically to be reminded of the dangers involved in such readings of
Hetty:

> Nature . . . has a language of her own, which she uses with
> strict veracity. . . . Nature has written out his bride's character
> for him in those exquisite lines of cheek and lip and chin, in
> those eyelids delicate as petals, in those long lashes curled like the
> stamen of a flower, in those dark liquid depths of those wonder-
> ful eyes.[21]

This ironic invocation of natural and iconic language is based not
only on physiognomy, as Fahnestock suggests, but on rhetoric.
The similes used to describe Hetty, the conventional flower metaphor, are all in a metaphorical sense, dead. Like Jenny's golden
hair, they belong more to the world of the viewer and the reader
than to Hetty herself. The frequent comparisons of Hetty with a
kitten, a peach, and a flower distract us from her body in the
same way that the Poysers and Adam are distracted from the signs
of her pregnancy. The sensuous vehicle of the metaphor over-
whelms the body it is meant to describe; language reproduces
language as Hetty reproduces and murders a child.

An alternative reading of the above passage reproduces Hetty
in another way. The flower metaphor, which usually suggests purity and innocence, is particularized, through the use of the sta-
men image, in a highly sexual way. The flower, then, like the
burning bush, becomes a way of both erasing and reproducing
sexuality, a way of suggesting Hetty's pregnancy in the language
of cliché. In this reading, the dead metaphor regenerates itself in
generating life and reproduces, not only a new vision of Hetty,
but a rereading of Dinah, who is, throughout, compared to a lily.
Hetty's sexuality gives birth to Dinah's; they are both linked with
the cycle of birth and death which become themselves metaphors
for the figuration that describes them.

While Eliot realizes the power of dead metaphor to regenerate

itself and to conceal its own regeneration, George Meredith sees
all potentially liberating uses of language as ultimately fatal.
Diana of the Crossways starts out with an invitation to decry the
"school box colors" most young ladies paint and are painted in:

> . . . transcribe from knowledge, show . . . flesh—facts, truer
> than the bone—fragrant with truth! And paint . . . the woman
> and the man, infuse blood, brains into the veiled virginal doll,
> the heroine.[22]

The novel begins with a sense of the erotic potential of language
to burn through cliché to what he calls "the naked body of truth."
Against this background, the heroine, Diana, wit, beauty, and
phrase-maker, would seem to have access to tremendous energy
and power. Like Mrs. Montecute Jones in *The Egoist*, she traps
other people in her own phrases; like Clara herself the very
unrepresentability of her own beauty grants her a certain exemp-
tion from the imprisoning powers of language. The first half of
the novel is a series of rhetorical victories for Diana; until she
falls in love with a man who is not her husband, her erotic and
emotional journeys are a series of experiments with language.

By the middle of the novel, however, it becomes clear that the
metaphors that are Diana's "refuge" are indistinguishable from
the dead "school-box" colors she rejects earlier. They are a product of sexual fall and inscribe themselves within a system of sexual
difference:

> Metaphors were her refuge. Metaphorically she could allow her
> mind to distinguish the struggle she was undergoing, sinking under
> it. The banished of Eden had to put on metaphors, and the com-
> mon use of them has helped largely to civilize us (*Diana*, p. 248).

All metaphor becomes dress to cover the naked body of truth;
Diana's body, which appears through fragments of her own writing at the beginning of the novel, necessarily disappears, becoming
enfolded in a series of conventional comparisons: once in love she
is a bird, a hunted animal, a flower, and herself a text. Women,
"the verbs passive of the alliance," remain inscribed in a patriarchal grammar that forbids the distinction between dead and
living metaphor.

The minimal possibilities for language rest for the novel, not in breaking through dead metaphor, but in creating a living being from dead parts. This nearly always occurs, in Meredith's novels, in communications between women. Lady Dunstane, Diana's best friend, receives a letter from her and

> read the letter backwards, and by snatches here and there; many perusals and hours passed before the shattered creature exhibited in its pages came to her out of the flying threads of the web as her living Tony [her nickname for Diana]   (Diana, p. 78).

Breaking into language shatters women; the price they pay for trying to move from cliché is fragmentation, synecdoche. The "school box colors" present women in an assumed wholeness, an integrity that depends on cover, dress, and disguise.

Synecdoche

It is, of course, in the nature of description to be synecdochal. No matter how committed to the realist enterprise, an author cannot name or describe every bodily part.[23] At some point the represented must come to stand for the unrepresented, the present for the absent. It is the intersection of the failure of language to fully represent, with a historical and political agenda, that concerns me here as elsewhere. In the Victorian novel, language fragments itself as it fragments the female body it undertakes to describe. The female body in the Victorian novel takes a particular shape that sketches itself out against the background of language's failure to represent. The bodily parts that comprise the litany which in turn constitutes the female body as it appears in the Victorian novel, are carefully selected not only for what they represent but for the absences they suggest. Like the "vital statistics" of the *Playboy* centerfold, the marked and selected attributes of the Victorian female body construct an imaginary body in the space between. Like these "vital" statistics, the eyes, brow, lips, hair, complexion, and "figure" of the Victorian heroine leave gaps for the production of sexual fantasy. *Playboy*'s inversion of the nameable and the unnameable, the represented and the unrepresented, inscribes itself in the rhetorical paradigms of Victorian realism; the Victorian novel aligns itself with *Playboy* in its sexual construction of the absent.

It would be a long, tedious, and doomed project to list the omissions in Victorian representations of the female body. Instead, this section performs the imitatively synecdochal operation of concentrating on presence to suggest absence; it detaches from the heroine's body the hair and the hand and arm, isolating and fetishizing these parts.

Victorian novels are frequently about women's hands: hands that stand for hearts, and hands that are won and offered by themselves. The hands that are offered with hearts, that represent in themselves something higher, constitute one of the centers of value in the nineteenth-century novel. They form a synecdochal chain where the heart represented by the hand is in itself a synecdoche for more obviously sexual parts of the body that enter into a heroine's decision about whom to marry. Asking for a hand is an entrance into the female body, the touch of a hand frequently the first touch between lovers. The disembodied hand, the hand without the heart and whatever it is that the heart itself stands for, is, in the terms of many Victorian novels, an unacceptable fragmentation of the female body. Lily Dale, her mother and sister must leave their uncle's house because they cannot let him "dispose of [their] hands" (Vol. II, p. 358). Lily cannot offer her hand to Johnny, after all her troubles, because she is a tree with a limb chopped off, a "fragment." The separation of her hand and heart makes her into a series of parts, an inadequate and unanswered synecdoche. Ultimately, without a "limb," she has no hand to offer.

The synecdochal chain shifts the burden of female sexuality away from the body as a whole, through the heart to the hand. It is according to the rhetoric of this shift that the Vicar of Bull-hampton can warn Carry Brattle away from prostitution by telling her to "keep her hands clean" so he can "find a place for [her] weary feet."[24] In the same way, the clue to Lady Audley's bigamy is her hand, the "ladies hand," or handwriting, that betrays her connection with the "dead" Helen and, more sinisterly, the bruise on her wrist that betrays her attempted murder of George Talboys.

In the case of Maggie Tulliver, the disembodied hand and arm are equally sinister synecdoches for the fully sexualized female body. Maggie's arms, as her aunt complains, "are beyond every-

thing"; Aunt Pullet's dress, to be made over for Maggie in time
for an evening party, cannot be altered enough to fit over Maggie's arms. As a consequence, Maggie wears short sleeves, and her
arms, visible to the world and the reader, become representative
for Stephen both of his desire for Maggie and of her desirability.
Barred from expressing his attraction to Maggie in any of the
conventional ways in which he is able, for example, to seek Lucy's
"hand," he catches Maggie alone at a dance and "showers kisses
on [her arm]."

> Stephen was mute; he was incapable of putting a sentence to-
> gether, and Maggie bent her arm a little upward toward the large
> half-opened rose that had attracted her. Who has not felt the
> beauty of a woman's arm? The unspeakable suggestions of tender-
> ness that lie in the dimpled elbow, and all the varied gently les-
> sening curves, down to the delicate wrist, with its tiniest, almost
> imperceptible nicks in the firm softness.[25]

Stephen's very incapacity to put "a sentence together" sets in motion a series of conventional linguistic operations, where the half-
open rose and the arm stand for the unspeakable. Stephen's gesture
exposes the link between synecdoche and fetishism; throughout
the rest of the novel, Stephen and Maggie will express desire, re-
luctance, and guilt with their arms. When Stephen calls on Maggie at her Aunt Glegg's they spend their time nervously taking and
dropping each other's arms; in the fatal boat trip we once again
recall the power of Maggie's arms as she is learning to row.

Maggie's inability to align hand and heart is ironically and sym-
pathetically worked out in the flood scene, where she dies with her
arms around Tom, in an embrace "never to be parted." Maggie's
embrace of her brother signals a psychological displacement that
echoes the displacements of language that articulate so many of
Maggie's experiences. In this final scene, her sexuality finds its expression in an erotic and fatal attachment to her brother, ironically, another man to whom, for reasons beyond her control, she
cannot give her "hand."

Maggie's sexuality, like that of many other Victorian heroines,
is announced not only by her arm but also by her "resisting mass"
of hair. Like the "wanton ringlets" of Milton's Eve, the hair of a
whole series of Victorian heroines comes synecdochally to repre-

sent their wantonness, their unnameable body parts. Hair is a particularly involuted figure because, like metaphor itself, it both covers and reveals, dresses and undresses the body. On the one hand,
like Eve's, the heroine's hair acts "as a veil down to the slender
waist."[26] On the other, it figures the body it hides. Dickens' Jenny
Wren, in trying to find out if Lizzie is in love with Eugene, loosens
her own hair and Lizzie's:

> Pretending to compare the colors and admire the contrast, Jenny
> so managed a mere touch or two of her nimble hands as that she
> herself, laying a cheek on one of the dark folds, seemed blinded
> by her own clustering curls to all but the fire, while the fine hand-
> some face and brow of Lizzie were revealed without obstruction
> in the sober light.[27]

This mitigated and manipulated letting-down of hair articulates
the double nature of the figure. Here hair acts as both screen and
clue to the natures of these two young women. Lizzie's hair both
suggests her sexuality and denies it; in thinking she is hidden by her
hair, Lizzie allows her attraction for Eugene to reveal itself. Jenny's
hair, which falls "in a beautiful shower over the poor [crippled]
shoulders that were much in need of such adorning rain" (p. 386),
both covers her deformities and allows her to freely fantasize about
the "Him" who will take her away from her mental and spiritual
pain.

Our Mutual Friend is Dickens' most self-conscious discussion of
synecdoche and fetishization of body parts. Almost everything in
the novel is reduced obscenely to its component parts. Lady Tip-
pins is made up completely of artificial bits and pieces: "You could
easily buy all you see of her in Bond Street: or you might scalp
her, and peel her, and scrape her, and make two Lady Tippinses
out of her, and yet not penetrate to the genuine article." The Ve-
neerings' butler, nicknamed the Analytical Chemist, hovers behind the novel's sumptuous dinner tables, appearing to be warning
everyone of what the food and drink are really composed of. Ve-
nus, Our Mutual Friend's bizarre spirit of love, makes up skeletons
from the assorted bones and organs of various people. Mr. Podsnap
imprisons his daughter and cuts her off from any communication
with the world by positing "a young person" who blushes at the
mention of anything even remotely improper: "Mr. Podsnap's

blushing young person [was] so to speak, all cheek: whereas there is a possibility that there may be young persons of a rather more complex organization." Young ladies at Podsnap's parties sit silently "comparing ivory shoulders." Dickens' consciousness of the particularizing nature of society, its tendency to break down and fetishize is itself personified/particularized in the young person's cheek, which comes to stand for a destructive and anatomized notion of femininity. Dickens tries to oppose to this vision of young womanhood one that is stronger and more integrated. Lizzie Hexam, who can run, row, swim, and carry an unconscious man, is an attempt at the fulfillment of such a vision. Throughout the novel, however, its three young heroines are repeatedly defined and confined by their hair. Bella is always proudly conscious of her curls; her playing with them is her identifying gesture. Lizzie and Jenny both repeatedly loosen their hair and screen themselves behind it; the young person, in Dickens' mind, then, becomes not all cheek—for that is hidden—but all hair.

The obsessive attention to hair as synecdoche explodes into melodrama in the sensation novels of the eighteen-sixties. Mrs. Oliphant's 1865 review of M. E. Braddon's works castigates her for making hair "one of the leading properties in fiction." In her summary of the various novels, Oliphant always includes a mention of hair, noting how one heroine's changes in the course of pages from "blue-black" to "dead-black" to "purple-black" and dwelling sardonically on another's "primrose coloured ringlets."[28] Oliphant concludes: "Remembering what she has written about Lady Audley's golden locks, we must admit that Miss Braddon is not given to admire any particular hue, and that she evidently loves hair for its own sake, providing that it is abundant (Oliphant, p. 97). The very abundance of the hair replicates the many levels of disguise and the multiple twists of plot that twine themselves around the female body in Braddon's novels.

Exaggerated as the language is with which Braddon describes hair, the hair itself is always real; in some sense it is always an icon of the true personality of the heroine. False hair announces itself as synecdoche and parodies its traditional role as indicator of sexuality. In *Jude the Obscure* Arabella's wig comes to stand for both sexual entrapment and a lack of genuine sensuality. In *He Knew He Was Right*, another bewigged Arabella, Arabella French, puts on and takes off her chignon as she tries to interpret whether her suitor, Mr. Gibson, wants a sensual sophisticated young woman or a simple country girl. Both Mr. Gibson and Arabella fetishize the chignon; to Gibson it is the embodiment of all that is ugly in Arabella:

> A man with a fair burden on his back is not a grievous sight; but when we see a small human being attached to a bale of goods which he can hardly manage to move, we feel that the poor fellow has been cruelly overweighted. Mr. Gibson certainly had that sensation about Arabella's chignon. And he regarded it in a nearer and dearer light—as a chignon that might possibly become his own, as a burden which one senses he might be called upon to bear . . . as a domestic utensil of which he himself might be called upon to inspect, and perhaps, to aid the shifting on and shifting off.[29]

When Arabella, in desperation, promises to do anything Mr. Gibson orders to get him to marry her, Mr. Gibson instinctively focusses on the chignon. To Arabella, and indeed to the French family, the chignon has come to represent beauty, fashion, and sexual attractiveness:

> And the whole French family suffered a diminution of power from the strange phantasy that had come upon Arabella. They all felt, in sight of the enemy, that they had to a certain degree lowered their flag. One of the ships, at least, had shown signs of striking, and this element of weakness made itself felt through the whole fleet   (*Right*, p. 374).

Both sides of this marital/marine battle invest Arabella's chignon with disproportionate meaning. By, in effect, pulling Arabella's hair apart from the rest of her body, Trollope focusses on it *as a* part, a metaphor for disproportion, a synecdoche.

Metatrope

The use of metatrope to imprison the female body and to distance it from the reader is embedded in the language of metaphorology itself. Paul de Man makes the connection between writing and painting as frames for women in his discussion of Locke's use of a female figure for rhetoric or eloquence ("Eloquence, like the fair sex, has too prevailing beauties in it to suffer itself ever to be spoken against. And it is in vain to find fault with those arts of deceiving wherein men find pleasure to be deceived").[30] De Man's commentary on Locke's figure shifts the focus of the discourse from writing to painting, from one metatrope to another:

> It is clear that rhetoric is something one can decorously indulge in as long as one knows where it belongs. Like a woman, which it resembles . . . it is a fine thing as long as it is kept in its proper place. Out of place, among the serious affairs of men . . . it is a disruptive scandal—like the appearance of a real woman in a gentlemen's club where it would only be tolerated as a picture, preferably naked . . . and hung on the wall.[31]

Both painting and writing are equally complicitous in this life-denying tradition of framing. Lock's metaphor inscribes itself in a tradition that associates written language with a fall from the assumed purity, innocence, and relative iconicity of spoken language.[32] The fall metaphor in turn throws into relief the figure of the fallen woman who comes to stand for rhetoric, ornament, manipulation, and insinuation—for all the seductions of language. De Man's metatropical shift reintroduces the naked female body more explicitly, while acknowledging the frame that makes its entrance into language "tolerable," even possible.

The conspiracy of writing and painting metaphors in the capture of female likeness becomes both subject and design in a number of Victorian novels. Perhaps the archetypal instance of this doubled capture is the presentation of Dorothea Brooke in *Middlemarch*. The opening paragraph of *Middlemarch* sets up the twin sign systems that repeatedly intervene between the reader's eye and Dorothea's physicality:

> Miss Brooke had that kind of beauty which seems to be thrown into relief by poor dress. Her hand and wrist were so finely formed that she could wear sleeves not less bare of style than those in which the Blessed Virgin appeared to Italian painters; and her profile as well as her stature and bearing seemed to gain the more dignity from her plain garments, which by the side of provincial fashion gave her the impressiveness of a fine quotation from the

Bible—or from one of the elder poets—in a paragraph of today's newspaper.[33]

This opening passage itself acts as a frame through which we must look at Dorothea and any subsequent clues about her appearance. Framed rhetorically by a system of metatropes and personally by a society that fails to interpret her correctly, she becomes herself a repository of canonical virtue, perhaps in her own physicality a "key to all mythologies." To understand the language that is Dorothea is to understand the novel in which she appears as a text.

Dorothea's body becomes a source of both sexual desire and philosophical debate. Will and Naumann each frame it according to the system of signs that seems most meaningful to them; to Naumann she is a potential model for his paintings, a counterpoise to the Ariadne, frozen in "a magnificent pose." Interestingly, his first act of artistic fantasy is to cover her body; "I would dress her as a nun in my picture" (*Middlemarch*, p. 198). Will's anger at his friend's presumption in wanting Dorothea as a model is revealed later when he tells Dorothea she is "a poem" (*Middlemarch*, p. 234). For Will, the *appropriate* act is the interpretation of Dorothea, her undressing; Naumann's arrogance lies in his desire to impose his interpretation on Dorothea. Dressing, therefore, becomes a more overtly sexual act than undressing. The capturing of likeness is a sexual act, but it is to Will specifically one of subordinating Dorothea to a larger, presumptuous "significance": "Yes," he says sarcastically, "and . . . your painting her was the chief outcome of her existence—the divinity passing to higher completeness and all but exhausted in the act of covering your bit of canvas. I am amateurish if you like: I do *not* think the whole universe is straining towards the obscure significance of your picture" (*Middlemarch*, p. 199). Will's uneasiness with the artistic "dressing" of Dorothea stems from his naive faith in the representational possibilities of language:

> Language gives a fuller image, which is all the better for being vague. After all, the true seeing is within; and a painting stares at you with an insistent imperfection. I feel that especially about representations of women. As if a woman were a mere coloured superficies! You must wait for movement and tone. . . . This woman whom you have just seen, for example, how would you paint her voice, pray?   (*Middlemarch*, p. 199).

Will presents language as an act of liberation, as an anti-frame that allows for "movement and tone." The "vagueness" of language permits a freedom not available to Dorothea through the double frame of the nun's dress and painting.

Will's discussion with Naumann is no abstract discourse on realism and representation. Representations of women are the mysterious exception, the proof of the failure of painting, the place where conventional discrepancies between signifier and signified are magnified into sexual trespass. The intersection of sexuality and realism casts questions on the nature of both; for Will, never the disinterested eye, Dorothea's capturing in painting is both sexual violation and an irredeemable error in representation.

Will's faith in language and the greater freedom he promises for his method of capturing Dorothea, his promise, perhaps, of greater mercy to the captive, speaks to the relativism of both his endeavors. He will be a better husband than Casaubon, he will represent Dorothea more fully than Naumann, he will provide Dorothea mitigated happiness and allow for her mitigated physicality.

Eliot's reservations about Will are closely and significantly linked to her reservations about the realist project. The "channels" which have no great name on earth in which Dorothea's "full nature . . . spent itself" are channels narrowed by the novel itself. In addressing herself half wistfully to an epic past, she frames the channeling of Dorothea's energies as a product of literary history:

> A new Theresa will hardly have the opportunity of reforming a conventual life, any more than a new Antigone will spend her heroic piety in daring all for the sake of a brother's burial; the medium in which their ardent deeds took shape is forever gone
> (*Middlemarch*, p. 427).

The power of reforming and reshaping is denied Dorothea, who must herself be formed and shaped. Compared constantly through figures of texts and paintings to canonical "originals," Dorothea is a faded copy, her body a carefully framed reproduction that must be "channeled" into a series of extended metaphors. The mitigated acknowledgment of her greatness frames Dorothea in the tempered rhetoric of realism.

A mirror-reading of *Middlemarch* does not merely invert or reflect existing codes. The mirror, as it appears in the novel itself is, as Eliot explains, a figure for egoism, which can also be read as a parable of writing itself:

> An eminent philosopher among my friends, who can dignify even your ugly furniture by lifting it into the serene light of science, has shown me this pregnant little fact. Your pier-glass or extensive surface of polished steel made to be rubbed by a housemaid, will be minutely and multitudinously scratched in all directions; but place against it a lighted candle as a centre of illumination, and lo! the scratches will seem to arrange themselves in a fine series of concentric circles around that little sun. It is demonstrable that the scratches are going everywhere impartially, and it is only your candle which produces the flattering illusion of a concentric arrangement, its light falling with an exclusive optical selection. These things are a parable   (*Middlemarch*, p. 247).

This passage, full of feminine allusions and displacements, applies most immediately to Rosamond and her egoism. As a parable for realism, however, it provides for the novel the missing point of view, the woman as subject rather than object, as framer and arranger, rather than the framed. The housemaid, pier glass, and domestic detail suggest the female point of view; the term "pregnant" to describe "fact" in the first sentence suggests the female body and Dorothea's own displacement of desire when she realizes for the first time that with her marriage, "The sense of connection with a manifold *pregnant* existence had to be kept up painfully as an inward vision instead of coming from without in claims that would have shaped her energies" (*Middlemarch*, p. 285; italics mine). The mirror, like Snow White's in Gilbert and Gubar's reading of it in the opening chapters of *Madwoman in the Attic*, becomes a source of both power and vulnerability, of vanity, and of introspection.

If Dorothea should become the candle, her body and experiences the focus for a series of concentric circles, the frames in which she is trapped begin to crack. To Dorothea paintings "are a language I do not understand. I suppose there is some relation between a picture and nature which I am too ignorant to feel" (*Middlemarch*, p. 81). Later, she explains more fully to Will:

> At first when I enter a room where the walls are covered with frescoes, or with rare pictures, I feel a kind of awe—like a child

present at great ceremonies where there are grand robes and pro-
cessions. . . . But when I begin to examine the pictures one by
one, the life goes out of them, or else is something violent and
strange to me. . . . That always makes me feel stupid. It is painful to be told that something is very fine and not to be able to
feel that it is fine—something like being blind when people talk
of the sky   (*Middlemarch*, pp. 215–16).

Dorothea's unconscious acknowledgment of the violence of her
framing is clear enough in the language in which she speaks of pictures. Her comparison of paintings to "ceremonies where there are
great robes" is both a statement of her fear of the sort of metaphoric "dressing" discussed in Chapter III and an instinctive answer to Naumann's proposal to dress her in nuns' robes. Being
framed for Dorothea is a matter of life and death; in her complaint that the life goes out of pictures upon examination, she is
speaking of the metaphoric death of her own physical desires. The
passage ends with an appropriately physical analogy, Dorothea's
attempt to articulate an unframed "natural" experience.

Dorothea's resistance to framing in this passage is carefully
coded; to step completely outside the role of painting would be
to upset the pictorial economy of the text. When Celia and Sir
James try to design a frame for her at the end of the novel by
placing her in the vicarious role of aunt to Celia's children, her escape, once again articulated in the language of painting, is equally
coded. Dorothea leaves Celia's home to face Casaubon's will and
her own sexual desires because "After three months Freshitt had
become rather oppressive: to sit like a model for St. Catherine
looking rapturously at Celia's baby would not do for many hours
in the day" (*Middlemarch*, vz. p. 111). Breaking out of her frame,
Dorothea is a painting come to life.

The act of unframing oneself, of stepping out of one's portrait,
is a subversive and dangerous move for women. Nineteenth-century
fiction in both Britain and America is haunted by paintings of
women coming alive. Poe's "Oval Portrait" and M. E. Braddon's
Lady Audley's Secret explore the terrible consequences of a portrait taking on life; in *Lady Audley's Secret* the portrait, a precursor perhaps of Dorian Grey's, takes on the burden of female evil
and sexuality and becomes more like Lady Audley than she is herself. Browning's painter poems as well as Tennyson's "The Lady

of Shalott" and the "Palace of Art" take up the theme of framing, narrative, and sexual control; the duchess who smiled too much is finally "painted on the wall" so her husband can control the recipients of her glances. Andrea Del Sarto's wife and model poisons his art; her only desire is to escape from his studio and paintings into the street where her "cousin" waits. The Lady of Shalott's breaking of her frame which is both portrait and mirror is a violent and self-destructive act that, in Tennyson's version, has terrible consequences for her own body and for the world of Camelot. The Pre-Raphaelite reframing of fictional women as paintings is, perhaps, an analogue to this fictively embedded framing process; the obsessive need to illustrate Victorian poems, including, of course, their own, is in itself an act of capture.

Since a frame can be protective as well as confining, its shattering can be a terrifying and confusing experience for the "model" as well as for the artist. In Trollope's *Last Chronicle of Barset*, both Conway Dalrymple, the portrait painter, and Clara Van Siever, the model he is simultaneously painting as Jael and trying to make love to, are uneasy about the possibility of moving beyond the security of their respective (framing) roles:

> The peculiar position in which he was placed probably made his work difficult to him. There was something perplexing in the necessity which bound him to look on the young lady before him both as Jael and the future Mrs. Conway Dalrymple, knowing as he did she was at present simply Clara Van Siever. A double personification was not difficult to him. He had encountered it with every model that had sat to him, and with every young lady he had attempted to win—if he had ever made such an attempt with one before. But the triple character . . . joined to the necessity of the double work, was distressing to him.[34]

If the fictive frame that surrounds Clara makes her unapproachable, it also reduces her to silence. Not realizing that Conway is stepping out of his role of artist into the role of lover, she answers his leading questions "without moving her face—almost without moving her lips" (*Barset*, p. 496). She has internalized her persona as Jael, and more important as subject; it is not she who can stop the painting and break the frame. This particular scene and frame are broken up by the comic intrusion of Clara's mother who, of course, sees the situation as it really is and marches Clara off in an attempt to force her to marry her own business partner. In this case the unframing of the model is relatively painless; framed itself by comic conventions, Conway and Clara's relationship survives and indeed thrives on her triple identity. In other Victorian novels, the outlook is bleaker, the stakes higher.

Dorothea's attempt to unframe herself is only half successful. While she can break free of her role as model, she cannot escape the larger frame of language. Susan Gubar has identified Dorothea as one of a series of "blank pages," or heroines who are acted upon, written upon, and shaped by inscriptions of male desire.[35] Like Rossetti's "Jenny" who is reduced first to textuality and then to a mirror upon which her clients carve their names with diamond rings, Dorothea, by becoming Will's "poem," becomes an inscription of *his* will, a text of his own making. Will's identification as a writer allows him hermeneutic control over Dorothea; his marriage to a poem gives him the privilege of interpretation.

Triply framed, as a painting, as a poem and as a character in the novel, Dorothea is imprisoned by the very concentric circles that arrange themselves around her; her point of view becomes at once focal and inaccessible. Other nineteenth-century novels use metatrope as a more isolated and perhaps more isolating strategy; women become pictures, sculptures, texts, or epithets in response to a particular need. Framing, unframing, and reframing become part of the act of reading, of inhabiting the fictive world of the novel; cameos of women's bodies appear and disappear.

Typically, metatrope has three important and sometimes overlapping purposes in the nineteenth-century novel. The first and most common is the distancing of the female body either by the narrator or a central male character at the moment of and as a reaction to its most intense effect. For the narrator, of course, this is the moment—or moments—of physical description, for the male characters, moment of physical attraction. The second strategy that centers on metatrope is repression, or self-framing on the part of the heroine to create a distance between herself and her own physicality. The last major use of this code is in itself metonymic; in this case the reading or interpretation of the heroine becomes a reading of the society in which she appears. The heroine is, in this case, the embodiment of a social or criminal problem, her body the clue to a mystery. Detective and sensation novels, which typically centered on a beautiful and enigmatic heroines are, of course primary examples of this use of metatrope.

Nowhere is metatrope more clearly used as a distancing strategy than in *Adam Bede* where, at crucial moments, Arthur Donnithorne erects a frame around his attraction to Hetty, presenting it as fictive and her body as a painting. In response to Irwin's questions about his intentions, Arthur explains, "I went to look at the pretty butter maker, Hetty Sorrel. She's a perfect Hebe; and if I were an artist, I'd paint her" (*Adam Bede*, p. 104). Arthur's explanation distances Hetty in a number of ways, first by the impersonal allusion to the pretty butter maker, then by the comparison to a classic tradition to which Hetty has no conscious access, and finally by the imposition of an artistic frame. The "if" of the second sentence suggests a second, unnamed alternative since he is in fact *not* a painter, which, taken in conjunction with the phallic nature of the paintbrush and Gubar's tradition of "blank pages," in turn suggest a sexual encounter. Irwine makes explicit the artificiality of the frame that Arthur provides:

> Well, I have no objection to your contemplating Hetty in an artistic light, but I must not have you feeding her vanity and filling her little noodle with the notion that she's a great beauty . . . attractive to a fine gentleman, or you will spoil her for a poor man's wife   (*Adam Bede*, p. 104).

Like Dorothea, Hetty is object, not creator; while it is proper to be looked at "in an artistic light" she must not herself aspire to artistic power and "make pictures" herself. Her own attempts at painting the future lead to her undoing:

> she thought of nothing that was present. She only saw something that was possible: Mr. Arthur Donnithorne coming to meet her again along the Firtree Grove. That was the foreground of Hetty's picture; behind it lay a bright hazy something—days that were not to be as the other days of her life had been
> (*Adam Bede*, p. 139).

The sinister effects of Arthur's painting metaphor become clearer as the novel progresses and Hetty is led to internalize his conception of her; in the two famous bedroom scenes, one before and one after the actual consummation of the affair, she frames herself, with the aid of a series of props, in her blotchy bedroom mirror.

Hetty's enactments of her pictures before the dark mirror attest both to the impossibility of her visions and to her powerlessness to create. Hetty's attempt at painting is appropriately aligned by Adam with images of sexual fall. When "in a sudden impulse of gaiety" she sticks the rose he gives her in her hair, Adam becomes sententious:

> That's like the ladies in the picture at the Chase; they've mostly got flowers or feathers or gold things i' their hair, but somehow I don't like to see 'em: they allays put me i' mind o' the painted women outside the shows at Treddles'on Fair
> *(Adam Bede,* p. 231).

Hetty's attempt to make herself into a picture is at once suspect; the connection between painting a picture and being a painted woman is direct and explicit in the class to which Hetty belongs. Any attempt to frame experience according to her own imagination is, by definition, sexual trespass.

Arthur's artistry in distancing himself and Hetty, their affair, and its consequences shapes the course of the novel. Hetty's body quite literally becomes too big for the frame in which he has carefully placed it. The failure of the frame to accommodate Hetty's growing body and desires signals to Arthur and to the world of the novel the terror of a painting come to life. Jocelyn Pierson, the sculptor-protagonist of Hardy's "Sketch of a Temperament," *The Well-Beloved*, employs Arthur's distancing strategy in his endlessly iterated search for his ideal woman. Jocelyn's "Well-Beloved" flits from woman's body to woman's body; "she who always attracted him, and led him whither she would as by a single thread, had not remained the occupant of the same fleshly tabernacle in her career so far."[36] Women's bodies, for Jocelyn, are at once merely vessels for the temporary containment of the Well-Beloved, and objects in themselves to be fragmented, fetishized, and, in the words of the novel, "translated into plaster" (*Well-Beloved*, p. 68). Clearly, Jocelyn's art is a form of sexual repression, a "translation" of desire into what the narrator perhaps appropriately calls "plastic." But there is more at work here, just as there is another pattern in Jocelyn's sexual life. Although notorious for his fickleness, Jocelyn does fall deeply in love—with three women: his childhood sweetheart, her daughter, and her granddaughter. The three[37] Avices are in

his words "perfect copies" of each other; Avice the first is reproduced physically if not spiritually in her incarnation as daughter
and granddaughter.

Jocelyn's love of women, then, is the love of women as they are
reproduced. He realizes his love for the first Avice only after she
dies and he studies an old photograph of her. Women unrepro-
duced, unrepresented, either by works of art or by each other, are
threatening, unerotic. Eroticism lies in representation; a painting
that stands for a woman, a woman that stands for another is a
less direct and therefore a less terrifying confrontation of female
sexuality.

In the second and final version of the novel, all three Avices
break through the frame he erects for them, break out of their
role as sculptures and into living sexuality. The first two Avices
marry other people; the third almost marries Jocelyn but runs
away at the last minute to marry a younger lover. Ironically, by
the end of the novel it is Jocelyn himself who is framed, reproduced, and denied life. The novel closes with a preemptive
epitaph:

> At present he is sometimes mentioned as "the late Mr. Peirston"
> by gourd-like young art-critics and journalists; and his productions
> are alluded to as those of a man not without genius, whose pow-
> ers were insufficiently recognized in his lifetime
>
> (Well-Beloved, p. 206).

Jocelyn lives on only in his productions; his life itself acquires an
artistic teleology that finds expression in epigram, in a reductive
narrative of his life and work. Jocelyn's framing in critical plati-
tudes is nothing short of murder.

Murder is doubly the consequence of artistic distancing in Tess
of the D'Urbervilles which can be seen as an extended attempt on
the part of the narrator, characters, and fate to frame Tess as a
text to be read, interpreted, and edited by her two lovers. From
the first, Tess' body is less that of an individual than the temporal
manifestation of a historical force. Tess' bodily fate is already
inscribed; its rape is a story repeating itself: "Doubtless some of
Tess D'Urberville's mailed ancestors frolicking home from a fray
had dealt the same wrong even more ruthlessly upon peasant serfs
of their time."[38] History and genetics mark Tess' body for further

marking; her "soft feminine tissue" is the blank page on which fate and an individual rapist converge to write their stories.

The textualization of Tess' body is itself a product of history and of industrialization. She belongs to two worlds; her body, so like her mother's, to a world of natural signs, icons, and folk superstitions, her mind to the educated world of "Sixth Standard English." Her body represents the transition of England from oral to written culture. Suddenly, Tess is readable, her face and body written evidence of her past.

Like Will Ladislaw, Angel is both Tess' liberator and her ultimate framer. Alex violently marks and scars Tess; Angel writes her story to reflect his desires. When Tess tremblingly tries to explain her past, Angel patronizingly inserts *his* interpretation of it: "My Tess has, no doubt, almost as many experiences as that wild convulvus out there in that garden hedge, that opened itself this morning for the first time" (*Tess*, p. 200). Angel's retreat to the conventional trope of flower deprives Tess of the power of language. The imbedded vulvar image in the name convulvus hints that Angel's use of the code may not be adequate to explain Tess' bodily history.

The arrival of the wedding day makes Tess more guilty and Angel more dependent on the metatrope of narrative. Her face becomes "a difficult passage" for him to "construe" (*Tess*, p. 248). Satisfied, however, that his reading of Tess is the only possible one, he ignores her repeated attempts to tell her story.

The wedding-night, traditionally the joining of two bodies, becomes a violent clash between two narratives. Angel tells his story and Tess responds with hers, which seems to her identical. Although the facts are similar, Angel's readings of his own and Tess' stories are vastly different. Tess is no longer a text he has written; she is a Jenny awakened, conscious and faithful to the experiences of her own body.

Angel will continue to misread Tess until the end of the novel. When she runs away from Alec, he looks for her under the wrong name, not understanding that he has forced her to return to her seducer. When she confesses that she has killed Alec, he once again takes refuge in textuality, in the possibility of the literary. He cannot see that her confession is not metaphorical: "What! Bodily!" he exclaims. The entrance of Alec's body as a replacement for metaphor is, codedly, the entrance of Tess' own. Throughout the text, Angel's allegiance to metaphor, his instinctual reference to trope and metatrope denies Tess the body that is her history.

Angel's transformation of Tess into text is an act of physical denial reiterated in the structure of the novel itself. In one sense, of course, the novel is Tess and Tess is the novel; her name and body give *Tess of the D'Urbervilles* its shape and meaning. The "Tess" of the novel's title is itself framed by the addition of her surname and its attendant configurations of family, history, and fate. The obsessively iterated symbolic patterns that provide a grid for the novel's actions, the constant use of red and white imagery, and the succession of scenes that foreshadow and repli-cate each other, form a textual net in which Tess' body is help-lessly enmeshed. The moments of Tess' nonalignment with the structuring principles of the novel, themselves deeply embedded and enmeshed, are moments consecrated to her body. Tess' hand in the milk pail at Talbothays is pink; the image resists the di-chotomy of red and white and presents us instead with a com-bination which is, aptly enough, flesh color.

While Hetty and Dorothea are framed as vivid paintings in oil, and Dorothea and Tess as texts that must be read, interpreted, and mastered, Lucy Snowe and Caroline Helstone live and love in the shadows of paintings of other women. In the novels in which they appear, they provide a sense of chiaroscuro, throwing other women into relief. Caroline, like Jane Eyre, is seen by her lover as fleshless; Robert, like Rochester, turns his denial of Caro-line's sexuality into the rhetoric of romance: "It appears you walk invisible. I noticed a ring on your hand this evening; can it be the ring of Gyges?"[39] Caroline's invisibility allows her vicarious par-ticipation in Robert's apparent romance with Shirley. She watches them as they walk from the top of a hill "like a bystander at a banquet." As she watches, she berates herself for her own invisi-bility, like Jane, trying to assert the presence of her bodily desires: "And what am I—standing here in shadow, shrinking into conceal-ment, my mind darker than my hiding-place? I am one of this world, no spirit" (*Shirley*, p. 383). Her words hauntingly recall Jane Eyre's, spoken at a time of physical and spiritual starvation: "I was a human being, with a human being's wants."

Caroline's very invisibility is translated into pictorial imagery. She is an "outline" or a "sketch" to Shirley's "Lovely picture of . . . incorrigible carelessness" (*Shirley*, p. 301), "she formed a picture, not bright enough to dazzle, but fair enough to interest; not brilliantly striking, but very delicately pleasing; a picture in which sweetness of tint, purity of air, and grace of mien, atoned for the absence of rich colouring and magnificent contour" (*Shirley*, p. 300). Caroline's constant comparisons to Shirley reflect her powerlessness in the novel. Quite literally in Shirley's shadow, her only hope is to become a picture in her own right. The happy ending with Robert is deliberately staged by Martin Yorke, a twelve-year-old neighbor who takes a fancy to Caroline because he and his sister have decided that Caroline "is like a picture in our dining-room, that woman with the dove in her hand" (*Shirley*, p. 174). When Martin despairs of Caroline's courage in arranging a rendezvous, he, ironically enough, hints at the liberating possibilities of Caroline's unframing: "She is not like our picture; her eyes are not large and expressive; her nose is not straight, delicate, Hellenic: her mouth has not that charm I thought it had. . . . What is she? A thread-paper, a doll, a toy . . . a *girl*, in short" (*Shirley*, p. 604). Martin's scorn simultaneously imprisons Caroline in metatrope—she has failed even in her role as picture—and suggests possibilities beyond the code. Caroline is, after all, a "girl," a word that both denies and betrays her sexuality. The "girl" in Caroline bursts through the idealizing frame of the painting; Caroline is not the sexless woman with the dove.

Caroline's romantic narrative ends within the confines of another painting. In finally confessing his love for her, Robert compares her to a picture of the Virgin Mary. The ending of *Shirley* with its promised banishment of fairies and other creatures of the imagination is stoically realistic, recalling the last pages of *Middlemarch*. Like Dorothea, Caroline's final appearance is as a copy of a powerful original.

Shirley's journey through the novel has a completely opposite teleology. The one-word title announces her unmitigated physical presence, even though she only appears a third of the way through it. She resists textuality, warning her lover Louis when he tries to read her physical symptoms, "Do not choose me for your text; I am a healthy subject" (*Shirley*, p. 517). Shirley is herself a writer of sorts; when she and Caroline take a walk through the fields on the day of the school feast, she envisions for her companion a prelapsarian Eve, bigger and more powerful than women of the present day. She answers Caroline's sanctimonious, "And that is not Milton's Eve, Shirley," conscious of her own powers of rewriting and reframing: "Milton's Eve! Milton's Eve! I repeat. No, by the pure mother of God, she is not! . . . Milton tried to see the first woman; but Cary, he saw her not" (*Shirley*, p. 328).

Shirley's visionary rewritings cannot sustain themselves; by the end of the novel her authorial voice speaks out only in schoolgirl compositions corrected and interpreted by her teacher/lover Louis Moore, to whom, like so many Bronte heroines, she defers as "master." Shirley's laziness robs her of authority and frames her as a text:

> If Shirley were not an indolent, a reckless, an ignorant being, she would take a pen . . . while the recollection of such moments were yet fresh on her spirit: she would seize, she would fix the apparition, tell the vision revealed . . . she would take a good-sized sheet of paper and write plainly out, in her own queer but clear and legible hand, the story that has been narrated, the song that has been sung to her   (*Shirley*, p. 398).

Shirley's "indolence" is no mere quirk of personality; her love for her schoolteacher, her willingness to submit to him in all things, and her inability to write are all part of the same inability to write her own unframed, unedited narrative. The novel's ending is bereft of fairies, of "apparitions" and of "visions" because Shirley's imagination is controlled and tempered, her pen inactive.

Villette's Lucy Snowe shares much in common with both Caroline and Shirley; like Caroline she is an "inoffensive shadow," a figure rendered invisible by "her robe grise," living a vicarious autobiography made primarily of the lives of other people. Like Shirley she takes her teacher as her lover. Lucy's narrative "I" is, seemingly, neither powerful nor self-assertive. The novel's title indicates her inability to shape the text to her name and body; its opening insistence on the drama of Paulina reveals her unwillingness to talk about herself. The one power she allows herself, however, is that of framing other women and resisting becoming a painting

herself. Lucy distances herself emotionally from Paulina by denying the little girl's physical presence. Paulina enters the text, through
Lucy's narrative "I" as a bundle and a shawl; she sees "signs and
tokens" of the child before she sees her. When Paulina cries out
for her father, she is an "it"; when she stands at her father's knee,
it "was a picture to see her."[40] Lucy herself scorns comparisons
with works of art, as we have seen in her refusal to take either the
Cleopatra or the painting series "vie d'une femme" as models for
her behavior. Paintings, self-proclaimed art, are suspect to Lucy.

Like Dorothea, Lucy escapes being framed as a painting only to
fall into textuality. From the beginning of her employ at the pensionnat, M. Paul is the reader of Lucy's face and body. Mme. Beck
commands him, as a physiognomist, to "read that countenance";
he answers without hesitation, "I read it" (*Villette*, p. 56). Although grateful for this particular reading that results in her being
offered a job, Lucy finds her role of text confining, his role as reader
a violation. Near the end of the novel, M. Paul boasts of his knowledge of the women of the pensionnat, Lucy of course included:
"My book is this garden; its contents are human nature—female
human nature. I know you all by heart" (*Villette*, 308). Lucy's
response, articulated in terms of Fall imagery, places M. Paul's
actions in the context of sexual trespass: "Monsieur, I tell you every glance you cast from that lattice is a wrong done to the best
part of your own nature. To study the human heart thus is to banquet secretly and sacrilegiously on Eve's apples" (*Villette*, p. 310).
M. Paul's readings of Lucy's character are transcriptions of his jealousy and possessiveness; his attention to her body and his transformation of it into text are simultaneously flattering and imprisoning for Lucy who resists being read to the point of sheltering vital
information behind her seemingly candid narrative "I." Lucy refuses transparency; she hides the fact that she recognizes Graham;
supplies us with an ambiguous ending to her tale, will not dress in
"transparent white dress." Her body and sexuality are at almost all
times hidden from the reader as she resists becoming a text in her
own autobiography. Lucy's revenge on M. Paul, her ultimate resistance to his reading, is her overtly textual double ending, where
she manipulates M. Paul's destiny and displays the power of her
own language. By the end of the novel, M. Paul is a pawn, an instant in her extended shipwreck metaphor. Her pen has the power

of figurative language; we do not know whether the storm that may or may not have taken M. Paul's life is "real" or metaphoric. She chooses to end her tale in doubt, wrapping up the fates of everyone but her lover. In the end, it is her narrative; hers the power of conclusion and control.

The act of hiding the body under the narrative "I" can be as much a strategy of repression as of power. Lucy's refusal to be read figures both a strong sense of narrative, bodily space, and bodily self-hatred. In *Jane Eyre* and in *Small House at Allington*, repression and self-assertion work hand in coded hand, expressing themselves through the medium of metatrope. Jane Eyre's self-portrait as "a governess, poor . . . and plain" is a triumph of repressive self-framing, at once a reminder and a denial of her body. The tropes with which she titles the picture provide a narrative second framing that makes access to the body doubly difficult. As a twice-framed governess, she cannot aspire to love Rochester. Jane's self-framing is, however, doubled in another way. By producing two paintings, one of Blanche and one of herself, she is, for all the differences between the mediums she uses, placing Blanche's desires in an equally fictionalized context. Like Lucy, Jane frames her rivals; in painting Rosamond's head she asserts control over another possible romance. In acting as both painter and painted, Jane preempts possible framing by Rochester; her self-portrait at once denies and inscribes her body.

Lily Dale undergoes a similar process of self-framing, although Lily uses language, not painting, to simultaneously imprison and express herself. In the course of the two novels that tell her story, *Small House* and *Last Chronicle of Barset*, Lily's name and body shrink, disintegrate, and vanish out of sight. We first see her as "Lillian Dale" then as "Lily Dale," as "L. D." and finally as "O. M.," the initials she writes in her diary that stand for "Old Maid." The shrinkage of Lily's name betokens a decrease in her physical and sexual presence; at the beginning of *Small House*, she is one of Trollope's most fully sexual heroines, pouring kisses on Adolphus Crosbie, scornful of acting "missish or coy." By the end of *Last Chronicle*, she is locked into a ritual refusal of Johnny Eames' proposals as he vows to send her an identically worded offer of marriage on the same day each year, while she continues to refuse him in a similarly formulaic way.

Lily's transcription of her erased sexuality in the initials "O. M."
is partially a reaction to her rivals', Madelina Demoines and Amelia
Roper, spiteful reduction of her to "L. D." Madelina uses these
initials in her flirtation with Johnny Eames; as the novel progresses, Johnny himself becomes complicitous in this reduction.
When Amelia coyly suggests that "L. D." is Johnny's mistress, he
jokingly claims that L. S. D. (pounds, shillings, and pence) are his
ruling spirits instead. Lily is transformed, then, from initial to cipher; like Jenny, she becomes a sign, a figure imbedded in a patriarchal economy.

By the end of *Last Chronicle*, Lily has internalized her narrative
framing and reproduced herself as "O. M." As elaborately illumi-
nated signs of sexual repression, the two initials that finally come
to represent Lily arrest her development as a human being. She
half-jokingly tells Grace Orley that at twenty-two she is one of the
"old women" of the neighborhood.

"O." and "M.," however, are not simply marks of repression. In
the economy of *Last Chronicle*, these ciphers themselves take on a
sexual value. The reason Lily finally rejects Johnny for the last
time in the novel is because Madelina has sent her an anonymous
letter in which she has enclosed a note from herself to Johnny,
signed, "M. D." Lily tries to banish the anonymous letter from her
mind, but fixates on the familiarity of "M. D.," which comes to
stand in her mind and Johnny's for sexual intrigue. By aligning it
with M. D., Lily's O. M. can be read as a similar indication of sexual desire embedded in denial.[41]

Reading or interpreting the framed heroine is never entirely an
individual act. The conventions that frame her, textual or paint-
erly, are themselves part of public discourse; interpretation itself
depends on convention, on some degree of cultural consensus. In
certain Victorian novels and poems where women are captured as
paintings or texts, however, the implications of interpretation are
more obviously social, less a strategy of personal distancing than a
means of understanding a culture or a problem.

The heroine's body figures prominently in a series of Victorian
texts that present a social or criminal problem; the body itself becomes a series of clues to solving a central mystery, the correct
reading of the body an answer to pivotal social questions. These
novels can be read as symptomologies where the reader's task is to

locate signs of cultural, political, or moral disease. In these novels the heroine's body is often marked or disfigured; it is a tissue upon which disease of some kind is violently and legibly traced. Lucy's body in *Dracula* has first to be read and then transcribed by Mina, who keeps and then types up a diary of Lucy's physical symptoms. By textualizing and interpreting Lucy, Mina is able to understand Dracula's crimes; her job as detective begins with a series of diary entries in which fluctuations in Lucy's physical appearance are carefully noted. Throughout the first part of the novel, Mina's journal catalogues the amount of blood in Lucy's cheeks—indicative of how long it has been since Dracula has visited—in the innocent language of tropical heroine description: "She has more colour in her cheeks than usual," "the roses seem to be coming back . . . to her cheeks," "she is still sadly pale and wan looking," "the roses in her cheeks are fading." Mina's prose subsequently explodes into a higher key as the implications of Lucy's lack of "roses" become life threatening, but for the first hundred pages of the novel, Lucy is textualized in a series of conventional tropes.

The mystery embodied by the heroine need not, of course, be criminal. *The Scarlet Letter* centers on the twin interpretation of Hester's body and the "A" that both represents it and covers it. Hester is, of course, an ambiguous text; although she cannot enter the town church because she finds herself the text of every sermon, the interpretations of her body, her experiences, and the scarlet "A" itself vary with time. The "A" that at the beginning of the novel stood simply, iconically, for "Adultery" comes to mean "Angel" by the end of the novel. Hester's body becomes at once an inscription of cultural values and a trace of the changes these values undergo with the passage of time.

If women's bodies are written transcriptions[42] of cultural problems, they are also, consciously or not, repositories of secret knowledge that must be processed to be understood. Laura Fairlie's face in Collins' *The Woman in White* is the unwitting answer to the mystery of Anne Catherick. Walter Hartwright, Laura's lover, her art teacher, and the amateur detective figure in the novel, takes the reader back in time to his first vision of Laura by describing, not her face and body, but a picture of her he drew in the first weeks of their friendship:

How can I describe her? How can I separate her from my own
sensations, and from all that has happened in the later time?
How can I see her again as she looked when my eyes first rested
on her—as she should look, now, to the eyes that are about to see
her in these pages? The water-color drawing that I made of Laura
Fairlie . . . in the place and attitude in which I first saw her,
lies on my desk as I write. I look at it, and there dawns upon me
brightly, from the dark greenish-brown background of the summer house, a light, youthful figure.[43]

The use of the drawing serves both to "separate" Laura from Walter's "sensations" and to freeze in space and time the body that the
reader must "see" in order to understand the novel. We must see
with Walter her hair, eyes, lips, and forehead, must share with
him in his conclusions. We must particularly see and understand
his contention that her face, "in a shadowy way, suggested . . .
the idea of something wanting," and we must finally be able to
compare the portrait of Anne Catherick, the "something wanting"
of the earlier description, with the "original." We must be able to
see how sorrow could transform Laura into Anne Catherick, both
for the mechanical purposes of plot and for a deeper understanding of the iterability and replaceability of women's bodies in the
novel.

   Like Lucy, Laura is watched, interpreted, and textualized by the
other female character in the novel. While Walter uses painting
to capture and understand Laura, her half-sister Marian uses language. Marian's journal, like Mina's, is a record of symptoms;
when Laura comes back from her wedding journey, Marian carefully takes notes:

   Others, who do not look at her with my eyes and with my recol-
   lections, would probably think her improved. There is more
   color, and more decision and roundness of outline, in her face
   than there used to be; and her figure seems more firmly set, and
   more sure and easy in all its movements, than it was when I look
   at her. . . . There was, in the old times, a freshness, a softness,
   an ever-varying and yet ever-remaining tenderness of beauty in
   her face, the charm of which it is not possible to express in
   words—or, as poor Hartwright used often to say, in painting,
   either (Collins, p. 201).

Sorrow marks Laura, making it more possible to capture her in writing and painting; the unfolding of the mystery simultaneously textualizes her and makes it imperative that she be interpreted. It is as if Laura's body with its firmer outlines is becoming a text in self-defense. This textualization is Laura's contribution to solving the mystery; Marian with her downy lip and masculine face, and Walter with his sexual interest in solving the mystery, must take the more aggressive, more traditionally male roles of interpreters and detectives.

In contrast to Laura's unconscious and helpful self-textualization, Lady Audley resists "capture" in any form of sign system, as she resists capture by the police by pleading madness. Robert's job throughout the novel is to textualize, to find evidence for, Lady Audley's true identity. Three major clues in this search and capture are her handwriting in a book she inscribes to her husband, George's letters describing his bride, and her Pre-Raphaelite portrait, which Robert and George must penetrate her bedroom through a secret passage to look at.

The inscription of Lucy's name in the book she gives in her earlier incarnation as Helen is an inscription of her physical identity. As Robert tauntingly puts it, a lady's "hand" never changes; writing transforms Lucy's physicality into a text that speaks against her. Similarly, the letters George writes to his sister, which include a minute physical description of his bride, give permanent shape to Lucy's body, enabling Robert to compare the two women physically. The painting is a more mystical act of capture; the figure it frames is really neither Lucy nor Helen, but the essence of both. The portrait moves beyond physical description in its reproduction of Lady Audley's body; by a Pre-Raphaelite exaggeration of physical detail, the painter paradoxically burns through the detail accumulated on the painting's surface:

> Yes, the painter must have been a pre-Raphaelite. No one but a pre-Raphaelite would have painted, hair by hair, those feathery masses of ringlets, with every glimmer of gold, and every shadow of pale brown. . . . It was so like, and yet so unlike . . . the perfection of feature, the brilliancy of coloring were there; but I suppose the painter had copied quaint medieval monstrosities until his brain had grown bewildered, for my lady, in his portrait

of her, had something of the aspect of a beautiful fiend (Braddon, p. 47).

By freezing Lady Audley for the time it takes to paint her hair by hair, shadow by shadow, the painter has come to recognize the many layers of her identity and to express them as a physical icon. The painting and the text provide the context in which Lady Audley and the mystery of the novel must be read and understood.

The Pre-Raphaelite painting that holds the secrets of Lady Audley's body is itself the icon of Victorian female sexuality, and itself articulates and amplifies the paradoxes of Victorian representation. Larger than life, emblazoned on the wall, the women in Pre-Raphaelite paintings are glowing emblems of female power and sensuality. Every hair takes on a life and a power of its own. The very dimensions of Pre-Raphaelite beauty and reproduction, however, are signs of what Peter Gay calls an "aesthetic of distance," a mythologizing that separates the Goddesses and heroines of the Pre-Raphaelite canon from the constraints of everyday life. On the one hand flamboyantly sexual, on the other, cloaked—even smothered—in layers of clothing, figuration and myth, Pre-Raphaelite paintings become at once the code of codes and the key to their unravelling. As the sexuality of the body is displaced onto the figure, the body itself, elusive and allusive, titillates by its absence.[44] The movement of displacement, of sexuality in motion between body and figure, is the moment of the reader's entry into the richness of Victorian representation.

Re-membering the Body: Contemporary Feminism and Representation

If Rossetti's "Jenny" embodies/figures Victorian representational coding, Rita Mae Brown's "Feminist" posits, in three lines, a mirror-world on the other side of Jenny's pier glass, where Victorianism and all its codes are banished:

> Having slumbered
> She rose and shook
> Victorian shadows from her hair.[1]

The "she" of "Feminist" might well be a Jenny wakened into consciousness and into the center of the poem; hers is the only action, the poem itself her unmediated territory which we see through her own, opened eyes. The guineas "Jenny"'s narrator places in her hair, signalling her victimization by and her complicity in a phallic economy, melt into shadows that are both sinister and insubstantial: sinister because they are tokens of a past in which a woman's hair was simultaneously a sign of her sexuality and a synecdoche that figured female dismemberment, and insubstantial because Brown, one of feminism's greatest optimists, has the bravado to suggest that this past and its signs can be shaken loose in a single physical gesture from the very symbol of its misogynist power. For the purposes of this chapter, the shadows, so easily shaken, are also symbols of Victorian representation itself; they are what stands between the reader/viewer and a clear perception of a woman's body. "Feminist" re-presents Jenny in representing a new kind of woman; she is the embodiment of a movement in her movement out of sleep and beyond the phallic gaze.[2] As Brown's signature replaces Dante Gabriel Rossetti's, and, perhaps more importantly, the names of the johns scrawled on Jenny's mirror, "Feminist" bravely dismisses the fascinations and dangers of Victorian representational coding and seems to produce a woman who can look into a mirror and see reflected there a face and a body unmediated by male desire.

If "Feminist" proclaims a hope for representation that is mythic in its power, its explanatory nature, and its implications for shaping culture, it also encapsulates a mythic view of history that provides a context for any discussion of feminist representation. In this poem, as in so many feminist texts of the so-called "second wave," Victorianism is directly opposed to feminism, which in turn becomes inscribed as a reaction to the repressiveness of the Victorian period.[3] Foucault parodies this binary view of Victorian "history" in his decentering of traditional sexual discourse, *A History of Sexuality*:

> At the beginning of the seventeenth century a certain frankness was still common, it would seem. . . . But twilight soon fell upon this bright day, followed by the monotonous nights of the Victorian bourgeoisie. Sexuality was carefully confined; it moved into the home. The conjugal family took custody of it and absorbed it into the serious function of reproduction. On the subject of sex, silence became the rule.[4]

Although Foucault, Peter Gay, and others[5] have attempted to rescue Victorianism from the charge of sexual silence, they do not deal primarily with the myth of that silence explicitly as it gives voice to twentieth-century feminism. This chapter is less concerned with feminist transformations of the erotic than with how these transformations affect the theory and practice of representation today, particularly the representation of the female body. I would argue that while the feminist movement in general has explicitly focussed on the subversion of Victorian mores, feminist literary theory and practice have defined themselves implicitly in opposition to Victorian representational coding. A major although not always articulated task of feminist writing has, so far, been the full and responsible representation of the female body, the breaking of codes and taboos that have trapped it in a "Victorian" past.

Karen Klein, "Eve," from the diptych "Eve and Adam," charcoal and pastel, 1985. Photograph by Ken Clark. With the kind permission of the artist.

While acknowledging both that representational coding of female physicality did not die with the body of Queen Victoria, and the work of feminist critics such as Sandra Gilbert, who have explored the "clothes" in which women's bodies were swathed during the intervening years, this chapter replicates feminism's rough outline of history in jumping from the nineteenth century to the beginning of feminism's "second wave" in the late nineteen-sixties.[6] Victorianism, its novels, poems, letters, and journals, have become the text for a variety of feminist critics; the fascination of authors as diverse as Caroline Heilbrun, Ellen Moers, Elaine Showalter, Nina Auerbach, Sandra Gilbert, and Susan Gubar with Victorianism is in part produced by and reproduces the centrality of the conflict between Victorianism and feminism. Just "outside" the field of literary study, feminist scholars have also centered on the Victorian period as a fertile ground for social history; historians and critics have combined to produce a series of enormous anthologies of Victorian women's "documents," such as letters, journals, transcripts of trials, and popular essays.[7]

The courtship[8] of feminism and Victorian studies is not merely the uneasy or convenient coupling of opposite terms. Feminism has so frequently found its texts, mirror images, and enemies in Victorianism because of the nineteenth century's ambiguous and erotic stance vis-à-vis the female body. While some feminist work denies this eroticism and others acknowledge it or at least bow to its possibility, clearly the fascination for the Victorian is in part erotically motivated. Victorianism and feminism become themselves a pair of tropes engaged in the kind of complex choreography described in earlier chapters.

Rhetorically, however, Victorianism remains the main enemy, the female body as it is represented in Victorian texts a straw woman, a wispy, insubstantial outline that it is the task of feminism to flesh out. Since the early nineteen-seventies, feminism has, in most of its manifestations, set out to do just that: to construct a female body in the face of patriarchal convention. It is no accident that *Our Bodies/Ourselves* should have become a central text for the early feminist movement, that reclaiming the body through reproductive freedom and analysis of rape, battering, pornography, and sexual abuse should have become central aspects of feminism, or that Robin Morgan should have concluded in the mid-nineteen-seventies that "the speculum may well be mightier than the sword."[9] Feminist artists of all sorts participated in this deconstruction of patriarchy and the construction of the body. In the art world, the struggle to represent the female body has been dramatically played out in the concept of "body art" which began with Georgia O'Keefe's vulvar paintings of flowers and is culminating today in the work of artists like Martha Wilson, Jacki Apple, Suzy Lake, and Ulrike Nolden Rosenbach, who dress their own bodies and present them live or on videotape to their "audience" *as* art.[10] In one room of Judy Chicago's Woman house, a woman sits before a mirror all day, making up her face, grimacing with dissatisfaction, and wiping it clean. Her face and her body are offered to visitors as a canvas over which she and society struggle for control. Body art is taken to its logical and violent extreme by the series of women artists who mutilate their own bodies in an attempt to portray the victimization and objectification of women.[11]

The works of feminist authors and critics become themselves an attempt to embody femaleness. Gilbert and Gubar focus on images of inner space and enclosure in women's writing, claiming that a sense of the spaces of the body provides a defense against phallic poetics.[12] Nina Auerbach claims the female body as a mythic territory, compressing the power of women's resistance to oppression into the huge and compelling figures of the women who haunt Victorian text; her Old Maids, Goddesses, Angels, and Fallen Women body forth female struggle, converting it into physical power.[13] Mary Daly, in her re-membering herstory of women's presence, locates the source of female potential in the body of the Hag which has traditionally been burned, bound, and dis-membered by patriarchy.[14] Elaine Showalter sees the history of feminism in terms of two images of the body; in sketching out a history of contemporary feminism, she embodies its chronology in the twin empowering metaphors of the Amazon and the mother.[15] Across the Atlantic, Hélène Cixous urges women to write the body, assuring them that "the more body the more writing"; Monique Wittig celebrates the female body in the figure of the Amazon and in her attempt to fully incorporate female physicality in her lists of bodily parts and fluids.[16] For these feminist critics and others, the body is at once the most literal ground of female experience and a metaphor for its very literalness.[17]

Feminist poetry has carved out a special place for the female body and takes a special place in the writing that struggles to represent it. Ntozake Shange explicitly grounds her writing in the body. She says, in her prefacing poem to *For Colored Girls Who Have Considered Suicide When the Rainbow Is Enuf*:

> My work
> Attempts to ferret out
> What I know I touch
> In a woman's body.[18]

Other feminist poets live precariously on the margins of representation, acknowledging both the impossibility of depicting the female body and the empowering need to try. Cynthia MacDonald's *W(Holes)* is a collection situated between these two positions and between the two meanings of the pun on "whole" and "hole": her poems are sketched out against the background of traditional poetics where women's bodies are both blanks and holes, their genitals both defining and absent, and project into the future a vision of wholeness, integrity, and representation. Leslie Ullman captures the same tension in "Undressing" where the act of taking off one's clothes, of shedding coding, reveals both body and blankness:

> I undressed for him,
> the room so familiar
>
> it contained no odors.
> The white walls,
>
> their shadows in place
> fell away, and my body
>
> emerged as space
> shaped like a body.[19]

Undressing replicates the movement of feminist representation, the moment of attempted depiction of the body. As language and "walls" fall away, what is revealed is both a body and the negation of a body; complete nakedness cannot be conjoined to complete presence as long as the undressing is "for him," a product of phallic language for the phallic eye.

This feminist poetry of the body places itself, predictably enough, in often loving and erotic opposition to Victorian representation. MacDonald exposes Victorian synecdoche in her re-membering of Florence Nightingale in "Florence Nightingale's Parts," while Sandra Gilbert's recent collection, *Emily's Bread*, attempts to move Victorian "types" such as the governess, the lacemaker, and the fallen woman from what she calls "daguerreotypes" into more fully representational poetry.

The feminist project of re-membering and incorporation produces a theory and practice that sees in Victorian representation a sinister mirror image, a distortion of the realities of female physicality. This chapter is the mirror of the others; it outlines feminism's attempts to break representational taboos and to focus on women's hunger, eating, and work. It looks at feminism's suspicion of metaphor, synecdoche, and cliché, and its attempts to circumvent them in a fuller re-presentation of the female body.

Throughout, the chapter looks at this attempt to break through the mirror of Victorian representation in two ways: first as a fertile and empowering project, and second as a way of writing and thinking that traps itself in the very codes it seeks to avoid or invert. What exists on the other side of the mirror can only be a mirror image; obsession with eating and hunger is as harmful to the body as starvation, attention to different parts of the body is still fetishization, metaphors for literalness are still metaphors. Feminist writers necessarily live and write at the center of a paradox; they are using patriarchal language to destroy patriarchy and the language it produces. To identify this paradox is not to recommend silence or stasis, but to identify conflict and contradiction as a potential source of energy.

In writing this "mirror chapter," I have taken advantage of one final inversion; I have switched my focus from novels and other prose genres to poetry. This is largely because, at this point in history, feminist poetry seems most nearly to embody feminist theory: many of feminism's theoreticians, from Adrienne Rich to Susan Griffin to Rachel Blau Du Plessis, are also poets in their own right. Many of the things I say about poetry could also be said about novels; Atwood's *Edible Woman* is as much a rebellion against strictures about eating as her prose poem "Simmering," discussed later in this chapter. Nora Ephron's *Heartburn*, like Ntozake Shange's "sassafras" challenges the hegemony of patriarchal form by "disrupting" its own text with recipes. Gail Godwin's novels are sometimes explicit rewritings of the lives and works of the Victorians; her *Odd Woman*, a "rethinking" of George Gissing's *Odd Women*, is only one case in point. In moving back and forth from the Victorians to the present, though it is cultural rather than generic tropes that concern me most deeply, contemporary feminist poetry provides the most accessible, playful, and serious attempt to shatter Victorian mirrors and to set up a world beyond Jenny's looking-glass.

Feasting on Eve's Apples

In appropriating the myth of the Fall and the female hunger that motivated it and set it in motion, feminist poets and artists[20] have celebrated women's relation to food and food's relation to sex, authority, creativity, and power. Erica Jong says of woman in "The Woman Who Loved to Cook" that "Even her poems were recipes." The poem celebrates female creative power, beginning with a mouth-watering list of foods that make Jong's own poem into a cookbook of sorts:

> Looking for love, she read cookbooks.
> She read recipes for *tartlettes*,
> *terrines de boeuf, timbales*
> & *Ratatouille*
> She read cheese fondue
> & *Croque Monsieur*
> & Hash High Brownies
> & Lo Mein[21]

In insisting that women's work and hunger are both sexual and textual, in allowing both her heroine to "read" cheese fondue and herself to write about it, Erica Jong subverts a series of taboos on the representation of women's hunger while maintaining its Miltonic and Victorian ties to power and authority. The heroine, "her breasts full of apple juice," can function in the absence of men: "no man appeared who could love her / . . . she would whip one up: / of gingerbread, / with baking powder / to make him rise." "Whipping" a man up is an act of violence and imagination, but also, importantly, a casual culinary chore. The first half of the poem is the woman's territory, her kitchen, the room of her own in which she can write her cooking. The second half answers the first by dissolving into couplets (and a couple): the heroine meets a man, "his cheeks brown as gingerbread, / his tongue a slashed pink ham," who "her friends predicted [would] eat her." The woman gets fatter, begins to drink, goes to a psychiatrist who "has read her book" and who pronounces her "Oral." The conclusiveness of the psychiatrist's pronouncement sets a frame around the heroine's power so succulently detailed in the first half of the poem. "Oral" dismisses her as a case of arrested development, a child, denying the very sexuality that empowers her cooking and her writing. The frame seems impenetrable, the psychiatrist's last words, "time's up," fatal, stultifying, life-denying.

The body of Jong's poem, however, resists the thrust of the psychiatrist's glib diagnosis; the richness and the weight of the poem lie with its first half; the second half, with its series of couplets introduced by "How does the story end? / You know it well," is itself a "recipe" for female self-destruction that reminds us of the tantalizing recipes of the first stanza. By constructing a poem that is a recipe in two senses and that employs all the forbidden senses, Jong creates/cooks up a poetics of female hunger. The psychiatrist who tries to "shrink" both head and body is impotent to shrink the body of the poem.

If recipes are a metaphor for female writing and hunger in "The Woman Who Loved to Cook," they explode into metaphors for the hunger and authority of black women in Ntozake Shange's "sassafras," which includes in the body of the poem a series of real "(kitchen-tested)" recipes:

> *sassafras' favorite spinach for mitch #10*
> 1–2 bunches japanese spinach
> 8 good sized mushrooms
> 2 tbn vegetable oil (safflower oil is very light)
> 2 tbn tamari sauce
> ¼ tsp finely crushed rosemary
> 4 sweet hot peppers
>
> wash spinach carefully in cold water. break
> leaves from stem with fingers. do not cut.
> sit in colander. wash mushrooms. slice
> vertically so each slice maintains shape. put
> oil in heavy iron skillet. heat til drop of

water makes it pop. turn flame down. lay
spinach evenly in pan. spread rooms.
sprinkle rosemary in tamari. simmer till
leaves are soft n hot. serve quickly. do not
overcook. place peppers around spinach in
nice design n serve.[22]

The "orality" of women's lives and writing is transformed in "sassafras" into black women's oral culture; the poem is punctuated according to the cadences of black speech. Recipes, lists of chores, and household rules, all intersect with and establish themselves as part of the "main narrative"; they are part of the life of the text in the way they are part of the lives of the women who write and live them. Categories of representable and unrepresentable are broken down as recipes become serious texts and serious texts subsume the playful punning forms of recipes. Hunger is central to the breaking of representational taboos; "sassafras" herself is a flavoring that spices up the form and texture of traditional white male poetic forms.

Both Jong and Shange focus on woman as cook, on her power to create, to generate and feed desire. Margaret Atwood shifts the terms of the problem of women and eating by parodying the Victorian association of particular foods with a particular gender. In her prose-poem "Simmering" she foregrounds the assumptions of texts like *Aristotle's Masterpiece:*

> For a while they worked it out that the men were in charge of the more masculine kinds of food: roasts, chops, steaks, dead chicken and ducks, gizzards, hearts, anything that had obviously been killed, that had visibly bled. The wives did the other things, the glazed parsnips and the prune whip, anything that flowered or fruited or was soft and gooey in the middle.[23]

It is a short step from the genderization of various types of edibles to the identification of womanhood itself with food. Several contemporary writers have replaced the Victorian association of women with dainty foods and sweets with the more empowering image of women as bread. The ending of Judy Grahn's Common Woman Poems, misquoted on T-shirts and postcards all over the country, sets up a structuring metaphor into which Sandra Gilbert plays in "Emily's Bread":

> No, now she is the bride of yeast,
> the wife of the dark of the oven,
> the alchemist of flour, poetess of butter,
> stirring like a new metaphor in every bubble.[24]

Emily Dickinson is both cook and bread, both writer and metaphor. She stirs the bread and is herself stirred. The bread image embodies another contradiction in Dickinson and in the Victorian woman in general; bread baking is the most acceptable of functions, but to become bread is to harness the power of rising and self-replication, the fecundity of yeast. While Grahn stresses the "commonness" of bread, the fact that it is necessary for physical survival, Gilbert focusses on its power as a metaphor for metaphors, its ability to generate language. The more marginal or luxurious foods accorded femininity in the Victorian era give way to the image of women as staples and as survivors.

Melanie Kaye explores the links between women, bread, and survival in "Jewish food: a process":

> She dreams about eating:
> baskets of bread sliced thin
> deep brown pumpernickel
> and rye, heavy with a thick crust.
> also challah and sourdough.
> she fills her plate, pickled herring
> and lox piled on parsley.
> she wants it all.
> she worries
> they think she's taking too much.[25]

The list of breads turns the poetic eye with its insistence on detail into an area that has, for women, been unrepresentable. The woman's uneasiness with her piling of bread onto her plate speaks to the larger problem of the woman poet and her "piling on" of unrepresentable detail. The title of Kaye's collection, *We Speak in Code*, addresses the problem of the poet's need to write codedly and the dangers attached to the violation of traditional rhetorical and poetic systems. For Kaye, feminism is the ability to acknowledge and portray female hunger; in "The Takeover of Eden," a utopian poem about the subversive potential of the dominant myth of female starvation, she describes night raids on Eden's trees: "Nights while they snore / we tiptoe through them, / stuff

fruit into our laughing mouths."[26] The last line of the equally utopian "Amazons" is a fantasy of female nurturance and support: "I
had never heard such / music. the village I knew, would be / un-
cluttered. they would feed me. / when I found the way."[27]

By inverting the myth of the Fall in one poem and, in the other,
positing a female world in which hunger is allowed expression,
Kaye is constructing a new mythology in which desire appears to
have a place. A number of feminist poets have looked to mythology to provide a place for their hunger and have replaced the patriarchal Fall myth with the at least partially matriarchal myth of
Ceres and Persephone. Poets like Rachel Blau Du Plessis, Louise
Glück, and Jane Creighton, as well as a series of science fiction
writers like Doris Lessing, Tanith Lee, and Joan D. Vinge, have
used the myth of Persephone to examine the question of female
appetite and to envision a female psychic universe. The myth, of
course, is in itself problematic; Pluto is both/either a rapist and/or
a means of awakening Persephone's own desire, while Ceres is
both/either a celebration of female bonding and unmitigated hunger (she is the goddess of harvest) and/or a complaining mother-
in-law whose function is the suppression of her daughter's sexuality. In Du Plessis' "Pomegranate," Persephone is identified with
the fruit, "Torn open— / that parchment of negative spaces"; the
hunger she must learn to acknowledge and to act upon is "a rid-
dle," "a taste of the mother," a hunger for her own body.[28] For
Du Plessis, as well as Milton, hunger is associated with speech and
power; it "speaks deep from the throat." The last two lines of the
poem make the connection between hunger, female sexuality, and
speech explicit:

> She knows that to speak
> she must swallow herself.

Persephone must desire her mother who is both her history and
the female body before she can break into speech. Like Du Plessis'
"Medusa," who must tell herself the history of her mother's rape
before she can form intelligible words (*Wells*, n.p.), Persephone
must tell of her own violation and her own desire in the same history, embody both these things in the same figure of her mother.
Hunger, both sexual desire and the swallowing of unpalatable
truths, is crucial to being able to speak and write.

Persephone's hunger and desire are differently, even oppositely
directed in Glück's "Pomegranate":

> First he gave me
> his heart. It was
> red fruit containing
> many seeds, the skin
> leathery, unlikely.
> I preferred
> to starve, bearing
> out my training.[20]

Told from the point of view of the daughter, the eating of the
pomegranate becomes an act of rebellion against starvation, the
transformation of the fruit into Pluto's heart, the displacement of
Persephone's desires onto language. The poem is, for the most
part, a recording of Pluto's rhetoric and actions. Persephone's only
recorded words—she "peers under" Pluto's arm to look at the
world above and to ask "What had she [Ceres] done with color
and odor"—are a questioning of maternal authority, which, in the
case of Ceres, Persephone interestingly equates with barrenness
and sterility. Glück's poem does not explicitly undercut Pluto's
arguments, and its final words are his:

> My dear
> you are your own
> woman, finally, but examine
> this grief your mother
> parades over our heads
> remembering
> that she is one to whom
> these depths were not offered.

Persephone's hunger, contained as it is within male rhetoric which
includes the ironic "you are your own woman, finally," is a hunger
for Pluto and the world he offers. Ironically, Ceres, goddess of the
harvest, cannot provide the food her own daughter needs.

Like Du Plessis and Glück, Jane Creighton locates Persephone's
hunger for the fruit in the larger context of women's hunger to
write. "Ceres in an Open Field" takes place before the rape; its
primary concerns, however, are Persephone's hunger and Ceres'

need to understand it. In Creighton's poem, Ceres wants to "write" her daughter "down exactly," and "record the bright colors/from her mouth."[30] Both the reference to color and the absorption with Persephone's mouth foreshadow the eating of the pomegranate and the disruption this will cause in the relationship between mother and daughter. In this telling, however, the colors that come out of Persephone's mouth, her desires and appetites, are what allow Ceres to write. In this version, mother tells the story of the daughter's hunger; the recontextualization of the Fall myth allows for the textualization of women's hunger.

The power of women to transform patriarchal cultural myths and to make a place for women's hunger is nowhere more clearly embodied than in Judy Chicago's *The Dinner Party*, a sculpture/ piece of art where women from all periods of history, goddesses, and female legends meet at one table to sit down to dinner. Forcing museums to make room for women's hunger and for the huge piece of sculpture has been a difficult task for Judy Chicago; *The Dinner Party* is so large it has no permanent resting place. Its mythic dimensions attest to the power of female appetite; its plates, individually designed by Chicago for every guest, attest, with their vulvar symbolism, to the linking of appetite for food to the erotic. *The Dinner Party* breaks through a number of phallic conventions; its size, subject matter, and incorporation of traditionally female "crafts" such as embroidery for the runners, make it a revolutionary piece that resists being swallowed by artistic convention, just as these women have resisted being "swallowed up by history." Muffled, hidden away in storage, *The Dinner Party* has become its own myth, defined and produced by female appetite.

If women's art embodies women's hunger, the appetites that make art possible in the first place produce the possibility of a feminist poetics. For French feminist Chantal Chawaf, the word itself is something that she "offer(s) . . . (to) be touched and eaten." The myth that she rewrites is psychoanalytic; by privileging the oral, traditionally framed as an "arrested" stage of development, she frees a part of the female body and of female developmental history to participate in the forbidden activity of writing for and with pleasure. "For me," she says, "the most important thing is to work on orality," to make viable, in language, women's childhood and early sexual experience. It is through the mouth,

through the celebration of the oral, that, for women, formative
sexual experiences can find an entrance into the text.[31]

Reworking the Body

Contemporary feminist discourse—critical and poetic—has attempted to absorb and transform the complex political and metaphoric structures that surround women's work in the nineteenth
century. By presenting women as workers, reclaiming the fallen
women, and resexualizing the mother, the artist, and the artist-as-
mother, contemporary feminism has once again held a mirror to
the Victorian representational tropes discussed in Chapters II
and III, producing an inversion that is startlingly reminiscent of
the images it reflects.

Adrienne Rich and Judy Grahn also write explicitly about
women's work; Rich's *The Dream of a Common Language* opens
with a poem about Marie Curie, which explores the link between
Curie's experiments with radium and her eventual death from
cancer. For Rich, the connections between female work and pain
are universal; all work leaves radioactive traces on the body, transforms it within and without. The differences between Rich and
the Victorian protectionist feminists who also saw work in terms
of its toll on the body is the connection between such transformations and power. She says of Curie:

> She died   a famous woman   denying
> her wounds
> denying
> her wounds   came   from the same source as her power[32]

Women's power under patriarchy comes only at a great physical
and psychic cost; its transformation into language, as the halting
lines and gaps between the words indicate, is equally painful—the
gaps themselves are scars and ruptures in the text.

The act of rupture involved in writing allows access to another
trace of work—the poet's craft. Rich celebrates the work of choosing words in "Cartographies of Silence," while simultaneously admitting their inadequacy and the pain that bringing them into
textuality involves: "Can I break through this film of the abstact/
without wounding myself or you/there is enough pain here."[33]

For Rich, the "abstract" that must be "broken through" is identified with metaphor and figuration, themselves the identifying
marks of patriarchal discourse. In "Natural Resources," she insists
on the literalness and, by extension, the reality and importance
of her subject. In describing the work of a female miner, she says:

> The miner is no metaphor. She goes
> into the cage like the rest, is flung
>
> downward by gravity like them, must change
> her body like the rest to fit a crevice.[34]

In resisting metaphor, Rich, along with many other feminists,[35]
aligns it with denial of the body. The miner's body, under patriarchal language, is "changed . . . to fit a crevice," as patriarchal
language is aligned with the physical violence of hard labor. The
abstract and the figurative distract the reader from physical reality;
feminist poetry becomes a reinscription of the literal.

Like Rich, Sandra Gilbert uses her poems to trace the marks of
work on the female body. Work transforms the governess of
"Daguerreotype: Governess" into the materials of her labor:

> Her eyes are darning needles, her breasts, pincushions.
> Between her thighs, icy as panes of glass,
> a thin ribbon of silk flutters and cries.
> There are no strong verbs in her sentences.
> (*Emily's Bread*, p. 37).

The lacemaker in the "daguerreotype" of that name "assumed the
shape / of a hook, its deft ferocity, / thin glitter and abstraction"
(*Emily's Bread*, p. 42). Elaine Scarry has noted how work scars all
laborers and how they become associated with the product and tools
of their particular kind of work;[36] the intersection of this representational tradition with the fragmentation of the female body
makes the female worker particularly vulnerable to the metonymic
shift where body becomes "tool."

Judy Grahn's famous "Common Woman" poems, a series of
seven "flexible, self-defining sonnets"[37] about working women, convey a similar suspicion of the abstract. Grahn's own introduction
to the poems claims that their popularity was "spurred by the en-
thusiasm of women hungry for realistic pictures." Women's hunger, like women's work, seems in Grahn's idiom to thrive on

"realism," on meticulous depiction of women who have traditionally found their place on the margins of representation. Although
each poem has its own structuring metaphor, each woman's life
connected with an image "that call[s] up various natural powers,"
the poems and the women in them survive on detail. "Ella, in a
square apron, along Highway 80" "slaps a wet rag at the truck
drivers / if they should complain. She understands / the necessity
for pain, turns away / the smaller tips, out of pride, and / keeps a
flask under the counter" (Grahn, p. 63). "Nadine, resting on her
neighbor's stoop / . . . holds things together, collects bail, / makes
the landlord patch the largest holes / . . . pokes at the ruins of the
city / like an armored tank" (Grahn, p. 65). Each detail in these
poems carries with it in its eruption into textuality a repressed, sup-
pressed, or forgotten moment of female experience.

Each woman, carefully located in time and place, carries with
her the work and experiences of other "common women" who live
in infinite but specific places, holding varied but specific jobs. The
"Common Woman" poems find themselves located in a collection of poetry which itself announces work as possibility and art;
in entitling the collection *The Work of a Common Woman*,
Grahn illuminates the connections between work, its depiction,
and female creativity.

Although work is not explicitly eroticized in Grahn's poetry,
Audre Lorde, in both her poems and essays, places work on a
continuum of female sexuality that includes "dancing, building a
bookcase, writing a poem, examining an idea."[38] The continuum
is familiar; nineteenth-century novelists, poets, and essayists saw
in the movement of women building, dancing, writing, and thinking, a trespass of carefully defined sexual boundaries. Lorde, like
the nineteenth-century protectionist, expands erotic space, drawing it out of the recesses of family and bedroom into public gesture
and discourse. Eroticism is both a by-product of and an impetus
to work. In her infinitely punning "recreation," Lorde connects the
work of artistic creation, the work of making/creating love, and
the playfulness of recreation in the interstices of more formal
"work":

> Coming together
> it is easier to work
> after our bodies

> meet
> paper and pen
> neither care nor profit
> whether we write or not[39]

It is both easier to work coming together after bodies meet paper and pen, and easier to work (presumably with paper and pen) after bodies meet. The very syntax, the way the sentences "work," announces an erotic energy that is both work and play, production and recreation.

Synecdoche: Writing the Good Parts

The recreation of the female body with its many zones of pleasure and playfulness depends on a respect for its integrity.[40] We have already seen how in Victorian literature and culture various parts of the body came to be fetishized sexually and representationally, as nameable, accessible parts of the body came to stand for the unnameable whole/hole. Twentieth-century sexual culture, the sexual "revolution,"[41] has produced an inversion of Victorian representational tropes, where the historically unnameable parts of the female body come to stand for the rest of it. The " 'vital' statistics" of the *Playboy* centerfold reduce her body and personality to three specific "zones," and then to numbers. The "breast men" and "leg men" of contemporary culture reduce women, like chickens, to nameable palatable parts. In hardcore pornographic magazines like *Hustler* and *Screw*, various more "bizarre" parts erupt into language and nameability, becoming themselves displacements for erotic pleasure; in the "all-Stump" issue of *Hustler*, for instance, "stumps" and prosthetic limbs replace traditionally conceived erogenous zones as sites of sexual attention.

Fetishism finds its objective correlative as much in "benign" cultural institutions as in pornography. Mary Daly identifies fetishism as a central component in the modern practice of gynecology and in the formation of women's self-image:

> At this point it is sufficient to note that the be-ing of women is condensed into particular parts / organs of her mind / body. A woman thus shrunken / frozen is manipulable / manageable. Her fetishizers feel potency / power which they otherwise lack, and ex-

ercise this negative and derivative potency to dis-place her energy
further and further from her center, fragmenting her . . . de-
vouring her. Dis-placed, she becomes a consumer of re-placements,
as in estrogen replacement therapy, cosmetic surgery, and psy-
chiatric re-placement of her Self-identified natural history by man-
made misinterpretations.[42]

Fetishism and synecdoche recall the power of presence by insisting
on absence; synecdoche foregrounds the gap between signifier and
signified, condensing the absences inherent in the production of
language.[43] Fetishization of particular body parts declares the rest
of the body to be absent in the very act of invoking it. Frequently,
sites of erotic pleasure are seen to be absences in themselves; the
"stumps" of the all-stump issue stand both for the female body
as a whole and for those parts that have been cut away from it.
The "cleavage" presented by culture as a requirement for fully
sexual womanhood is an absence in itself, a "hole" that mimics
the perceived absence of female genitalia and a denial of the
"wholeness" of the body.

Feminist poets and theorists have been concerned with representing the falseness and fragmentation of traditional depictions
of women, and replacing them with more integrated representations. Du Plessis' "Breasts" is an early identification of the problem
of synecdoche; the poem, which follows a woman as she walks
through a city street, looks carefully at the fragmenting gazes of
the men who watch her walk. "Breasts" is full of parts, made up of
the bits and pieces of women which the male point of view allows the reader to see; one man carries a sawed-off hand in a brief-
case; two other men pass a breast between them. The woman comes
into physical presence in the poem as a gap between parts, a
moving absence that produces gazes but which is not in any way
reproducible as presence.[44]

Adrienne Rich's "To a Woman Dead in Her Forties," is a poem
about silences, absences, and fragmentation—finally, a requiem
to synecdoche. An elegy to a woman who died of breast cancer,
the poem's first line, "Your breasts /   sliced-off," contains in
its very arrangement on the page the gaps that reduce female sexuality to the unrepresentable. Against the background of silence and
hesitation produced by both the gaps and the text of the poem, the
narrator writes, "I'm half-afraid to write poetry / for you   who

never read it much / and I'm left laboring / with the secrets and the silence." The word "breasts" with its attendant slash is both a reminder of women's sexuality and of the fact that it exists in language only because it has been cut off.[45] The naming of "breast" is a revolutionary act for women who have never spoken of their sexuality or touched each other; it is made possible by an eruption into language that in its violence sacrifices a part of the body.[46]

Feminist attempts to inscribe female physical integrity in a language that is made up of parts of their bodies take different forms at different historical moments and in different locations. Olga Broumas and Monique Wittig try to insert pressed parts of the female body into representational gaps. In her poem, "Artemis," Broumas experiments with the creation of a language that can represent traditionally unrepresented parts of the female body:

> I work
> in silver the tongue-like forms
> that curve round a throat
>
> an arm-pit, the upper
> thigh, whose significance stirs in me
> like a curviform alphabet
> that defies
>
> decoding, appears
> to consist of vowels, beginning with O[47]

The "curviform alphabet" replicates and contains the female body; by "defying decoding," it resists the usual fragmentation of language—it is a closed, curved "O-shaped" system that replicates the original sounds of human speech. This language and its alphabet, which are inseparable, are, in fact, Origin, the beginning, the real place of women that begins with the details of their physical experience. Women's existence begins / originates with this alphabet, begins with "O."

By focussing on parts of the female body traditionally unrepresented either before or after the sexual revolution and the revolutions of language it produced, Broumas is creating for the female body a place separate from culture, near the origin, near the beginning that is an "O." Broumas' bodily parts provide a context for erogenous zones, a more diffuse locus of sensuality.

Monique Wittig reiterates Broumas' move in her novel *The*

Lesbian Body, whose narrative is regularly punctuated by a series of female bodily parts in capital letters, arranged with spaces in between. Wittig's list encompasses and curves around the whole female body; she lists traditional erogenous zones, organs, bodily fluids, parts of the skin. In breaking up distinctions between inside and outside, "erogenous" and "other" (the lists seem to be in no particular order), she insists on the integrity of the female body, on the interdependence of its parts, and on the necessity for these parts to create a space for themselves in language. The spaces between the words are loci for parts of the body she herself has left out or forgotten, the spaces between cells and organs, the cavities of the body.

Other French feminists, like Hélène Cixous and Luce Irigaray, have located female representation in women's reproductive organs; these, for them, are the sites of "difference" and of cultural repression. For Cixous, "there is always within [woman] at least a little of that good mother's milk. She writes in white ink."[48] Cixous looks at the phallocentric poetics described by Gilbert and Gubar through a mirror, replacing male with female genitalia as the "organ of generation." Luce Irigaray, while contending that "woman has sex organs just about everywhere," uses the two lips of the vagina as synecdoches for women's feeling of division and "otherness" condensing what she calls the "diversified . . . geography of her pleasure" into a single (double) location.[49]

Even women's doubleness, potentially a source of originality, fecundity, and subversion for Irigaray, is strangely singular. Madeleine Gagnon, a lesser-known contemporary of Irigaray and Cixous, sees man's power as being located in his twin identities: "he is constantly double, he and his phallus."[50] While for Gagnon "man" and "phallus" are analogous terms, each with a separate if parallel identity, woman is absorbed, for Irigaray into the doubleness of the two lips that are not so much analogies as synecdoches for her sexuality and her existence. Gayatri Spivak dislocates women's creativity from the uterus and other reproductive organs to relocate it in the clitoris, the site of pleasure (*jouissance*).[51] Writing the body is the marking out of specific bodily territories, the privileging of a certain set of signifiers in a metonymic political and sexual chain. Kristeva's argument that "woman" no longer means woman but is simply a name for the unrepresented and repressed of patriarchal culture is only one step further along the chain, where woman herself becomes a synecdoche for representation.[52]

In resituating the "nameable" parts of women's bodies, in changing the Victorian meaning of "good parts,"[53] from hands, feet, and hair to the reproductive organs, the French feminists have replicated, by inversion, the fragmentation of Victorian representational coding. In choosing the reproductive and/or sexual organs as the site of meaning and desire in female writing, they replicate the conventions of pornography, the coerciveness of cleavage, the absence at the center of female sexuality as it is reproduced in phallic culture. The Whole of female sexuality reduces itself to a "hole," to the invagination or the negative folds within a female text.[54]

The Body Literal

Feminist suspicion of metaphor is, of course, only a synecdoche for feminist mistrust in and dis-ease with patriarchal language in general. From the Wyf of Bath to Anne Elliot to Adrienne Rich, the heroines and female writers who people feminist critical history have discovered and made public their discomfort with patriarchal language as a medium for the representation of women, their experiences, and their bodies.

Many feminists find themselves in the tradition of St. Augustine, claiming for metaphorical language a doubled distance from the origin, the signified, the authoritative truth.[55] Metaphor, frequently seen as "dressing" or ornament by mainstream linguists, has for many feminists from Charlotte Tonna to Audre Lorde to Rich, seemed to be a sinister "covering" of the female body. This tradition of resistance to metaphor, the "flower" of poetic language, has found its way into feminist poetry and poetics. Rich's resistance to metaphor in her description of the miner is replicated throughout the feminist canon. Anne Sexton begins the second wave of resistance with her insistent lines in "Menstruation at Forty": "the womb is not a clock, nor a bell," and then, in a similarly resistant syntax, about her uterus:

> They wanted to cut you out
> but they will not.

> They said you were unmeasurably empty
> but you are not.
> They said you were sick unto dying
> but they were wrong[56]

The uterus cannot be summed up by patriarchal metaphors, diagnosed and described by the terms of male doctors; it resists language, defies encasement. In trying to depict a female physicality free of patriarchal structure, Sexton disrupts traditional notions of poetic propriety; in his eulogy at Sexton's funeral, Robert Lowell diagnosed Sexton's rhetorical madness, recommending her retextualization: "Many of her poems would have been fascinating if someone had put them in quotes, as the presentation of some character, not the author."[57]

The depiction of the uterus, of explicitly female bodily parts and functions, becomes, for Sexton, the occasion of resistance to the patriarchal language that will allow woman's body only a limited or framed place, or no place at all. Similarly, in Adrienne Rich's "Sibling Mysteries," the "mystery" of reproduction becomes itself a metaphor for origin and for literalness. The two sisters in the poem are "translations / . . . of a text still being written / in the original";[58] their appearance in language can only translate their physical and literal existence.

Audre Lorde has a double stake in resisting white male language, and a double approach to metaphor. In her collection of poems, *The Black Unicorn*, Lorde invites a figurative reading by producing the figure of the black unicorn and using it as a title for the first poem in the collection. The black unicorn at once announces itself as an enigmatic symbol and resists a metaphoric reading:

> The black unicorn is greedy.
> The black unicorn is impatient.
> The black unicorn was mistaken
> for a shadow
> or symbol.[59]

By linking "shadow" and "symbol," Lorde is stressing both the blackness of the unicorn and the connection between blackness and the signs and tokens of white phallic economy. If women figure in this economy as signs, as tokens of exchange, blacks are even more obviously a commodity. Black women bear the double burden of prostitution and slavery, are doubly symbolic, doubly removed from "literal" and complete depiction. Lorde reminds us of the inadequacy of representation in "Walking Our Boundaries" when she says, "it does not pay to cherish symbols / when the substance / lies so close at hand / waiting to be held / your hand / falls off the apple bark / like casual fire / along my back."[60] The repetition of "hand," the pun on it, contrasts the sensuality of touching with the abstractness of "symbols."

For some feminists, language and metaphor hold the possibility of re-formation.[61] For Mary Daly, patriarchal language and the metaphors that uphold it are all dead, "faded" and "sleepy." The task of feminist philosophy and feminist language is to infuse life into dead metaphor, to re-infuse it with color, to awaken it into "gynergy." In her parodic "Edward the Dyke," a short prose poem about a lesbian who goes to a psychiatrist to be "cured," Judy Grahn has Edward speak in the language of phallic representation. When the psychiatrist asks what "the word 'homosexuality' means to you, in your own words," she has none; they are all borrowed from heterosexual convention. Edward is a metaphoric grave-robber:

> Love flowers pearl, of delighted arms. Warm and water. Melting of vanilla wafer in the pants. Pink petal roses trembling overdew on the lips, soft and juicy fruit. No teeth. No nasty spit. Lips chewing oysters without grimy sand or whiskers.[62]

This overflowering/overflowing of metaphor denies the body, the teeth, spit, and whiskers that Monique Wittig celebrates as rightful components of the lesbian body. In a similar parody of metaphorical suicide, a cartoon in the Radical Lesbian pamphlet, *Love your Enemy?*, shows a lesbian poet/singer with a guitar. The caption reads:

> I will now sing a short song comparing my lover's clitoris to a pearl, and her labia to a persimmon fruit and her vagina to a vanilla pod because quite frankly that's the only way I can cope with it all.[63]

The search for literalness and mistrust of metaphor becomes especially complicated as they intersect with the question of lesbianism. In her response to Catharine Stimpson's essay on lesbian literature in the "Writing and Sexual Difference" issue of *Critical*

Inquiry, Jane Gallop comments on Stimpson's definition of lesbianism:

> At the beginning of her article on the lesbian novel, Catharine R. Stimpson states that her "definition of the lesbian will be conservative and severely literal." We are prepared for the nonrhetorical, a shift from literary metaphor to sexual fact. It turns out that the "severely literal" is the domain of the body. . . . Political sympathy and affectionate friendships are excluded from the literal definition, however severe we might find that exclusion. They are only figuratively or symbolically lesbian. Literal lesbianism is "a commitment of skin, blood, breast and bone."[64]

Gallop focusses on two vital issues here: first, the metaphor of literalness somehow residing within the (female) body, and, second, the inevitability of highly metaphoric language ("a commitment of blood, breast and bone") at the moment of her most "severe" literalness. As the ultimate breaking of phallic taboos, lesbianism becomes a test case, lesbian writing the possible final moment of rupture with figuration. Lesbianism itself generates metaphors, as we see in Stimpson's attempt at a "severe" definition, and *is* or can be a metaphor, as we see in Adrienne Rich's essay, " 'It is the Lesbian in Us . . . ,' " which, as the title suggests, posits a lesbianism in all women which does not require the "literal" "commitment of skin, blood, breast and bone."[65] Since lesbianism can (metaphorically) be seen as the replication, doubling, or intensification of the female body, it follows that literalness associated with the female body be itself doubled/replicated by lesbianism. This equation is of course itself metaphoric and depends on the twin metaphors of "the literal body" and "the literal lesbian." Stimpson's listing of bodily parts is both metaphor and synecdoche, her definition of the "literal lesbian" a synecdoche for lesbians in general.

The production of metaphor can take place without the phallus; phallic structures can/must develop parthenogenically from the bodies and texts of women. Mary Daly would suggest that writing or loving between women gives birth to a new kind of metaphor, unfaded, unsleepy, a "live" birth. This formulation, unabashedly metaphoric, promises a space outside history, outside the bodies in which women are constrained to live. Ultimately, it envisions language as a tool for getting beyond language, and metaphor as a way of getting beyond metaphor to an "elemental," primary, and finally, literal truth.[66]

The alignment of women with the literal, the "original"[67] and the primal intersects historically with women's writing as a necessary realism and ties them to a mimetic tradition that reflects and is reflected by women's traditional role as "mirror" for others.[68] This mirror, like Snow White's, like Dorothea Brooke's, and like the one feminists hold up to patriarchy only to invert it, must also be shattered, if women are to be free to create in the way they please.

In the attempt to produce and to reproduce the literal female body, contemporary feminists have only succeeded in creating a metaphor. For many feminists, the female body has become a figure for literalness and truth, for a realism that is faithful to women's experience of themselves. Thus enveloped in meaning, the body has taken on mythic and empowering significance that derives in part from the denial of its own figurative richness.

Full representation of the body is necessarily impossible in a language that depends for meaning on absence and difference, and literal representation impossible in a language that is itself a metaphor for thought. The work of Jacques Lacan tells us, furthermore, that a totalized body is not only rhetorically but psychically inaccessible; since our knowledge of the self is constituted in and by discourse, we can only construct for ourselves a body in pieces, a *corps morcelé*. Literary representation, then, is not the process through which the body is fragmented; the fragmentation has already occurred and is always already reoccurring in the necessary and constitutive encounter with the mirror.[69]

Within this system of rhetorical and psychic gaps and figures, the outline of the female form is constantly shifting, blurring, and taking on new and temporary historical definition. Feminist attempts to subvert particular codes or taboos have inscribed themselves within the very conventions they reject; the battle against synecdoche has reproduced and replicated synecdoches, the fight for literalness has produced metaphor, the struggle to awaken "dead" metaphors or clichés has produced a string of representational corpses.

This does not mean that the struggle to reject phallic representational codes has not been of great historical importance, and that the metaphor of the literal body is not compelling or empowering. The impossibility of reaching beyond phallic discourse, of righting and unwriting phallic proportions, foregrounds rather than denies the importance of the feminist struggle to disrupt language. Anything that foregrounds the inequities of representation, even if this is an admission of the impossibility of moving into a safe space beyond it, is feminist; anything that struggles against these inequities is essential.

Notes

Notes to Introduction

1. See Steven Marcus, *The Other Victorians: A Study of Sexuality and Pornography in Mid-Nineteenth-Century England* (New York: Basic Books, 1964); Martin Meisel, *Realizations* (Princeton: Princeton U. Press, 1983); Nina Auerbach, *Woman and the Demon* (Cambridge: Harvard U. Press, 1982; and Peter Gay, *The Bourgeois Experience: Victoria to Freud: Education of the Senses* (New York: Oxford U. Press, 1984).

2. For examples of women's inability to use bodily language, see Elaine Showalter, *A Literature of Their Own: British Women Novelists From Bronte to Lessing* (Princeton: Princeton U. Press, 1977), pp. 26–27.

3. Michel Foucault, *The History of Sexuality Vol. I*, Trans. by Robert Hurley (New York: Random House, 1980). Francis Barker, *The Tremulous Private Body: Essays on Subjection* (New York: Methuen, 1984).

4. Leonard Barkan, *Nature's Work of Art: The Human Body as Image of the World* (New Haven: Yale U. Press, 1975).

5. See, for example, Bernie Zilbergeld, *Male Sexuality* (New York: Bantam Books, 1978), pp. 1–2.

6. Gayle Rubin, "The Traffic In Women: Notes on the 'Political Economy' of Sex" in *Towards an Anthropology of Women*, Rayna R. Reiter, ed. (New York: Monthly Review Press, 1975), pp. 157–211. Elizabeth V. Spelman, "Woman as Body: Ancient and Contemporary Views," *Feminist Studies*, Vol. 8, No. 1 (Spring 1982), pp. 109–31.

7. Annette Kolodny, *The Lay of the Land: Metaphor as Experience and History in American Life and Letters* (Chapel Hill: U. of North Carolina Press, 1975).

8. Jacques Derrida, "White Mythology," *New Literary History*, Vol. 6, No. 1 (Autumn 1974), p. 44.
9. Delores Rosenblum, "Christina Rossetti: The Inward Pose," *Shakespeare's Sisters: Feminist Essays on Women Poets*, Sandra M. Gilbert and Susan Gubar, eds. (Bloomington: Indiana U. Press, 1979), pp. 82–98. Betsy Erkkila, "Greta Garbo: Sailing Beyond the Frame," *Critical Inquiry*, Vol. VII, No. 4 (June 1985), pp. 595–619.

Notes to Chapter I

1. For scenes in which men's dinners are discussed in detail see, for example, Trollope's description of Mr. Kennedy's stingy offerings in *Phineas Redux* (New York: Oxford U. Press, 1973), p. 86; the after-dinner fight over wine in *The Prime Minister* (Oxford: Oxford U. Press, 1973), p. 88; or the detailed description of Plantagenet Palliser's abstemious dinner (*Prime Minister*, p. 55).
2. Henry Mayhew, *Voices of the Poor*, Anne Humphreys, ed. (New York: Frank Cass & Co., Ltd., 1971), p. 74.
3. Sandra M. Gilbert and Susan Gubar, *The Madwoman in the Attic* (New Haven: Yale U. Press), pp. 53–59, 273–74, 345.
4. Countess _____, *Good Society* (London: George Routledge and Sons, 1869), p. 114.
5. Eugene Beckland, *Physiological Mysteries and Revelations in Love* (Philadelphia, 1845), p. 29.
6. Mary Wood-Allen, M.D., *What A Young Girl Ought To Know* (London, The Vir Publishing Co., 1905), p. 89.
7. M. E. Braddon, *Lady Audley's Secret* (New York: Dover Publications, 1974), p. 129.
8. Gilbert and Gubar, p. 149.
9. E. D. E. N. Southworth, *Self-Raised or From the Depths* (New York: G. W. Dillingham, 1897), p. 142.
10. Aristotle (pseudonym), *Aristotle's Master-Piece* (New York: Company of Flying Stationers, 1811), p. 45.
11. Anorexia has often been seen as a sign of an awkward transition to womanhood. See Marlene Boskind-Lodahl, "Cinderella's Stepsisters: A Feminist Perspective on Anorexia Nervosa and Bulimia," *Signs*, Vol. 1, No. 1 (Winter 1976), pp. 342–55.
12. Elizabeth Robbins Pennell, *The Feasts of Autolycus: The Diary of a Greedy Woman* (London: John Lane, 1896), p. 157.
13. Mrs. H. O. Ward, *The Young Lady's Friend* (Philadelphia: Porter & Coates, 1880), p. 162.
14. Marian Harland, *Eve's Daughters, or Common Sense for Maid,*

Wife, and Mother (New York: John R. Anderson and Henry S. Allen, 1883), p. 111.

15. Dinah Mulock Craik, *A Woman's Thoughts About Women* (London, 1858), Chapter six.
16. Quoted in Nina Auerbach, "Alice and Wonderland: A Curious Child," *Victorian Studies* (September 1973), p. 40.
17. *The Bazar Book of Decorum* (New York: Harper & Brothers, 1870), p. 193.
18. C. Willett Cunnington, *Feminine Attitudes in the Nineteenth Century* (London: William Heinemann, 1935), p. 84.
19. Hilda Bruch, *The Golden Cage: The Enigma of Anorexia Nervosa* (Cambridge: Harvard U. Press, 1978), pp. vii–ix.
20. Elizabeth Gaskell, *Cranford/Cousin Phillis* (New York: Oxford U. Press, 1972), p. 26.
21. Marina Warner, *Alone of All Her Sex: The Myth and Cult of the Virgin Mary* (New York: Alfred A. Knopf, 1976), p. 74.
22. Barbara Ehrenreich and Dierdre English, *For Her Own Good: 150 Years of the Experts' Advice to Women* (New York: Doubleday, 1979), p. 109.
23. *Eight Cousins* is also the book in which Alcott makes her most critical statement on fashion: Rose tries on two costumes, one of a fashionable young lady, and one that her mentor/uncle has designed. The latter is loose and comfortable; the fashionable one, tight and unhealthy. Rose is tempted by fashion but ultimately decides in favor of health and her uncle.
24. Quoted in Mirabel Cecil, *Heroines in Love: 1750–1974* (London: Michael Joseph, 1974), p. 49.
25. Mrs. A. Walker, *Female Beauty* (London: Thomas Hurst, 1837), p. 168.
26. See, for example, Lucy's victory over Griselda Grantly in *Framley Parsonage*, and Fanny's victory over Julia Brabazon in *The Claverings*.
27. From *Godey's Lady's Book* (1860), rpt. in Cecil, p. 100.
28. Charlotte Bronte, *Life and Works Of The Sisters Bronte*, Volume VI (London: Haworth edition, 1899), p. 145.
29. For a discussion of illness as power, see Caroll Smith-Rosenberg, "The Hysterical Woman: Sex Roles in Nineteenth Century America," *Social Research*, Vol. 39 (Winter 1972), pp. 652–78.
30. Trollope entitles the chapter in which this occurs: "Miss Staveley Declines to Eat Minced Veal." The title itself suggests a code; readers were evidently supposed to be able to gauge Madeline's frame of mind from this information.
31. Charlotte Bronte, *Life and Works*, VII, p. 280.

32. Elizabeth Gaskell, *Wives and Daughters* (London: Knutsford edition, 1906), p. 202.
33. Charlotte Bronte, *Life and Works*, VIII, p. 236.
34. George Eliot, *Works*, VIII (Boston: 1886), p. 427.
35. Lewis Carroll, *Alice in Wonderland* (New York: W. W. Norton, 1971), p. 43.
36. Auerbach, "Alice and Wonderland," p. 41.
37. See Gilbert and Gubar's discussion of Victorian women writers' obsession with the Fall myth in Chapters 6, 12, and 16.

Notes to Chapter II

1. Barbara Ehrenreich and Dierdre English, *For Her Own Good: 150 Years of the Experts' Advice to Women* (New York: Doubleday Books, 1979), p. 114.
2. Anthony Trollope, *The Way We Live Now* (New York: Harper & Brothers Pub., 1875), p. 12.
3. Wanda Fraiken Neff, *Victorian Working Women* (New York: Columbia U. Press, 1929), p. 56.
4. Florence Nightingale, *Cassandra* (Old Westbury: The Feminist Press, 1979), p. 26.
5. Dinah Mulock Craik, *A Woman's Thoughts About Women* (Philadelphia: B. Peterson and Brothers, 1856), p. 15.
6. Anna Jameson, *Communion of Labor* (London: Longmans, Brown, Green, Longmans and Roberts, 1856), p. 27.
7. Louisa May Alcott, *Work* (New York: Shocken Books, 1977), p. 67.
8. Linda Gordon and Ellen DuBois, "Seeking Ecstasy on the Battlefield: Danger and Pleasure in Nineteenth Century Feminist Sexual Thought," *Feminist Studies*, Vol. 9, No. 1 (Spring 1983), p. 7.
9. I am using Elaine Showalter's definition of the Victorian female canon as my own. She says: " 'Residual Great Traditionalism' . . . has reduced and condensed the extraordinary range of English women novelists to a tiny band of the 'great,' and derived theories from them. In practice, the concept of greatness for women novelists often turns out to mean four or five writers—Jane Austen, the Brontes, George Eliot. . . ." *A Literature of Their Own* (Princeton U. Press, 1977), p. 7.
10. Anne Bronte, *Agnes Grey* (Edinburgh: John Grant, 1924), p. 54.
11. Unsigned review, *The Athenaeum* (December 25, 1847).
12. Charlotte Bronte, letter to W. S. Williams, December 21, 1847.
13. Charles Dickens, *Dombey and Son* (New York: Oxford U. Press, 1974), pp. 242–43.

14. Jane Austen, *Emma* (New York: Oxford U. Press, 1923), p. 85.
15. Sandra M. Gilbert and Susan Gubar, *The Madwoman in the Attic: The Woman Writer and the Nineteenth-Century Literary Imagination* (New Haven: Yale U. Press, 1979), p. 521.
16. George Eliot, *The Mill on the Floss* (New York: Oxford U. Press, 1980), p. 319.
17. Charlotte Bronte, *Life and Works*, VII, pp. 113–14.
18. Elizabeth Barrett Browning, *Aurora Leigh* (London: The Women's Press, Ltd., 1978), Bk. I, 1, 380.
19. For a discussion of female bodily imagery in *Aurora Leigh*, see Cora Kaplan's introduction to the above edition.
20. George Eliot, *Works*, VII, p. 31.
21. Elizabeth Gaskell, *North and South* (New York: Oxford U. Press, 1973), p. 131.
22. *Fraser's Magazine* was among the first to expose the unfair expectations of governesses revealed by such advertisements. In one article it described governess advertisements as requiring "such a catalogue of literary, ornamental, and moral acquirements as one would think no ordinary mortal would lay claim to" (Neff, p. 160).
23. M. Jeanne Peterson, "The Victorian Governess: Status Incongruence in Family and Society," in Martha Vicinius, ed., *Suffer and Be Still* (Bloomington: Indiana U. Press, 1972), p. 10.
24. Lady Blessington, *The Governess* (Philadelphia: Lea and Blanchard, 1839), p. 31.
25. Charlotte Bronte, *Life and Works*, VI, p. 192.
26. George Gissing, *The Odd Women* (London: 1893), p. 25.
27. Michael Hiley, *Victorian Working Women: Portraits from Life* (Boston: David R. Godine, 1979), p. 11.
28. Thomas Dublin, *Women at Work* (New York: Columbia U. Press, 1979), p. 77.
29. Charlotte Tonna, *Works*, VI (New York: M. W. Dodd, 1847), p. 402.
30. Nina Auerbach has suggested a connection between Ruth's sexual illness and venereal disease.
31. T. J. Edelstein, " 'They Sang the Sons of the Shirt': The Visual Iconology of the Seamstress," *Victorian Studies*, Vol. 23, n. w. (Winter 1980), p. 183. Edelstein does not point out that almost none of the seamstresses in her study is depicted in the act of working.
32. Cartoon from *Punch*, by John Tenniel, July 4, 1863.
33. Thomas Hardy, *Tess of the D'Urbervilles* (New York: W. W. Norton, 1979), p. 74.

34. George Eliot, *Works*, VI, p. 86.
35. Hardy makes his views on Tess' innocence quite clear in his discussion of her self-condemnation: "But this encompassment of her own characterization, based on shreds of convention . . . was a sorry and mistaken creation of Tess' fancy. . . . It was they that were out of harmony with the actual world, not she. Walking among the sleeping birds in the hedges, watching the skipping rabbits on a moonlit warren . . . she looked upon herself as a figure of Guilt intruding into the haunts of innocence. But all the while, she was making a distinction where there was no difference" (pp. 72–73).

Notes to Chapter III

1. D. G. Rossetti, "Jenny," line 286.
2. For a discussion on women as blank pages, see Susan Gubar, "The Blank Page" and the issues of Female Creativity," in Elizabeth Abel, ed., *Writing and Sexual Difference* (Chicago: University of Chicago Press, 1982), pp. 73–93.
3. George Eliot, *Works*, VI, p. 21.
4. Elizabeth Gaskell to an unknown correspondent, September 25 (1865?) in J. A. V. Chapple and A. Pollard, eds., *The Letters of Mrs. Gaskell* (Cambridge: Harvard U. Press, 1964), Letter No. 505.
5. "Ruth," unsigned article, *North British Review*, XIX (1853), p. 91.
6. Mary E. Dewey, ed., *Life and Letters of Catherine Maria Sedgwick* (New York: Harper and Brothers, 1871), quoted in Ann Douglas Wood, " 'The Scribbling Women' and Fanny Fern: Why Women Wrote," *American Quarterly*, Vol. XXIII (Spring 1971), p. 6.
7. Charlotte Tonna, *Works* (VI), p. 11. Elizabeth Gaskell, *The Life of Charlotte Bronte*, pp. 237–38, quoted in Frederika Brenner, *The Woman Question in Mrs. Gaskell's Life and Works*, p. 59.
8. Elizabeth Gaskell, Letter No. 515 (above).
9. Dinah Mulock Craik, *A Woman's Thoughts About Women* (Philadelphia, 1856), p. 56.
10. Marian Harland, *Eve's Daughters* (New York, 1883), p. 326.
11. Barbara Leslie Epstein, *The Politics of Domesticity: Evangelism and Temperance in Nineteenth Century America* (Middletown, Conn: Wesleyan U. Press, 1981), p. 78. Marian Harland, *Eve's Daughters*, p. 99.
12. *Englishwomen's Review* (December 1876), anthologized in Janet

Murray, ed., *Strong Minded Women and Other Lost Voices from 19th Century England* (New York: Pantheon Books, 1982), p. 270.

13. Anon., *My Secret Life*, Chapter 2, quoted in Fraser Harrison, *The Dark Angel: Aspects of Victorian Sexuality* (New York: Universal Books, 1977), p. 273.
14. Elizabeth Barrett Browning, *Aurora Leigh*, Book I, lines 1098–99.
15. George Eliot, *Daniel Deronda* (London: Blackwood, 1876), Book VII, p. 20.
16. Fraser Harrison, *The Dark Angel: Aspects of Victorian Sexuality* (New York: Universal Books, 1977).
17. Ronald Pearsall, *The Worm in the Bud: The World of Victorian Sexuality* (Harmondsworth: Penguin Books, 1983), p. 323.
18. Anthony Trollope, *The Vicar of Bullhampton* (New York: Dover Publications, Inc., 1979), pp. v–vi.
19. Monique Wittig, *The Lesbian Body* (New York: Avon Books, 1982), p. i.
20. The dressing of prostitutes in language, the conscious replacement of body by sign, has its novelistic roots in the works of Daniel Defoe whose overtly sexual heroines would seem, at first glance, to be the very embodiment of the gaps in Victorian writing. Nancy Miller argues that *Moll Flanders* can be read as feminist narratology, "practicing a theory of the female text." Certainly images of menstruation, childbirth, and prostitution generate from Moll's personal experience and structure Moll's narrative which forms the greater part—the body—of the novel.

    Although Moll's voice and body do dominate the middle portion of the text—those places where her vibrant "I" speaks directly through the reader—her narrative and therefore her body are framed by an enclosing, even imprisoning, text in two parts—the "Bookseller's Preface" and the conventional redemptive ending. The preface is most relevant here; in a narrative that threatens to reproduce a prostitute's body, Defoe has arranged that the preface reform, reframe and redress the problem of Moll's language:

    > It is true that the original of this story is put into new words, and that the stile of this famous lady . . . is a little alterred, particularly she is made to tell her own story in modester words than she told it at first . . . All possible care . . . has been taken to give new lewd ideas, no immodest ideas in the new dressing up [of] this story (p. 3).

    The "dressing" of Moll's body and story in "modester words" posits, of course, the existence of a naked, erased text that would

somehow capture the realities of Moll's experience. This text is
Moll's body which, like Jenny's, is imprisoned in a larger, more
culturally sanctioned text that takes the form in one case of a
poem and in the other of a novel.

21. Charles Dickens, *Oliver Twist* (New York: Oxford U. Press,
1966), p. 323.
22. Delores Rosenblum: "Christina Rossetti: The Inward Pose,"
Shakespeare's Sisters: Feminist Essays on Women Poets (Bloomington: Indiana U. Press), pp. 82–98.
23. For a discussion of metaphor as journey from home, see Jacques
Derrida, "White Mythology," *New Literary History*, Vol. 6, No.
1 (Autumn 1974), pp. 44–45, 55, 73.

Notes to Chapter IV

1. Anthony Trollope, *The Small House at Allington* (New York:
Dodd, Mead and Co., 1906), p. 71.
2. William Dean Howells, *Heroines of Fiction* (New York: Harper,
1901), p. 97.
3. Howells himself extends forward as well as backward in time. See
the extended parody of Howells' realism by Alice Wellington
Rollins, "Effie's Realistic Novel," reprinted in *American Realism:
A Shape for Fiction* (New York: Capricorn Books, 1972), p. 112.
4. Mary Cowden Clarke, *The Girlhood of Shakespeare's Heroines*
(London: Bicker and Son, 1864, Vol. I), p. 110.
5. See, for example, Jacques Derrida, *Of Grammatology* (Baltimore:
Johns Hopkins U. Press, 1976), pp. 27–44.
6. There are two noteworthy collections of essays on the theory of
description: a special issue of *Yale French Studies, Toward a
Theory of Description* (New Haven: Yale U. Press, 1981), and
Marc Eli Blanchard, "Description, Sign, Self-Desire" (The Hague:
Mouton, 1980).
7. Philippe Hamon, "Rhetorical Status of the Descriptive," in *Towards a Theory of Description*, p. 7.
8. See Jeanne Fahnestock, "The Heroines of Irregular Features:
Physiognomy and Conventions of Heroine Description," *Victorian
Studies* (Spring 1981), pp. 325–350, and Michael Irwin *Pictur-
ing: Description and Illusion in the Nineteenth Century Novel*
(London: George Allen and Unwin, Ltd., 1979).
9. See discussion of Charlotte Tonna on pp. 53–54 of this study,
and Adrienne Rich, p. 139.
10. I take the term "choreography" from the interview with Derrida
by the same name because it most aptly described the sense of

play, movement, and sexuality I see at work in Victorian culture. The term, however, is not entirely appropriate since it suggests a choreographer, someone who has consciously mapped out and controlled the movement.

11. For the classic reading according to codes, see Roland Barthes, *S/Z* (New York: Hill and Wang, 1974).
12. See Donald Davidson, "What Metaphors Mean," in Sheldon Sacks, ed., *On Metaphor* (Chicago: U. of Chicago Press, 1979), p. 30, for metaphors as dress.
13. For metaphor as "Scandal," see Umberto Eco, "Scandal as Metaphor," *Poetics Today*, Vol. 4, No. 2 (1983), p. 217. Nelson Goodman also frames metaphor in the imagery of sexual fall by his identification of it as "moonlighting" on p. 175 of *Metaphor*. There are many more examples.
14. See Jacques Derrida, "White Mythology," *New Literary History*, Vol. 6, No. 1 (Autumn 1974), pp. 44–45; 73.
15. For a discussion of what it would mean for feminists to kill "the angel in the house," see Sandra M. Gilbert and Susan Gubar, *The Madwoman in the Attic* (New Haven: Yale U. Press, 1980), p. 17.
16. For the connection between painting and murder, see Delores Rosenblum "Christina Rossetti: The Inward Pose," cited in Chapter III.
17. Mary Shelley, *Frankenstein* (New York: Oxford U. Press, 1969), p. 34.
18. M. E. Braddon, *Lady Audley's Secret* (New York: Dover Press, 1974), p. 6. I am indebted, for a discussion of Lady Audley as angel, to my student, Julie Zisk.
19. Mrs. Henry Wood, *East Lynne* (Boston: Baker, n. d.), p. 11.
20. Elizabeth Gaskell, *Works*, VIII, p. 371.
21. George Eliot, *Works*, VI, p. 158.
22. George Meredith, *Diana of the Crossways* (New York: Random House, n. d.), p. 18.
23. For an exhaustive attempt to represent the body by listing body parts, see Monique Wittig, *The Lesbian Body* (New York: Avon Books, 1980). I discuss this in Chapter V.
24. Anthony Trollope, *The Vicar of Bullhampton* (New York: Dover Publications, Inc., 1979), p. 161.
25. George Eliot, *The Mill on the Floss* (New York: Oxford U. Press, 1980), p. 388.
26. John Milton, *Paradise Lost*, Bk. IV, 1, 304.
27. Charles Dickens, *Our Mutual Friend* (New York: Harper, 1865), p. 157.

28. Mrs. Oliphant, "Sensation Novels," *North British Review,* 43 (1865), pp. 97, 99.
29. Anthony Trollope, *He Knew He Was Right* (New York: Dover Publications, Inc., 1983), p. 364.
30. John Locke, *An Essay Concerning Human Understanding* (Bk. 4, Chapter 10, pp. 105–106).
31. Paul De Man, "The Epistemology of Metaphor," in *Metaphor,* pp. 13–14.
32. For a parody on the fall into writing, see George Stade, "*Parole* into *Ecriture*: A Response to Murray Krieger," *Boundary* 2, Vol. 8, No. 1 (Fall, 1979), p. 124.
33. George Eliot, *Works,* VII, p. 5.
34. Anthony Trollope, *The Last Chronicle of Barset* (Boston: Houghton Mifflin Co., 1974), p. 496.
35. Susan Gubar, "The Blank Page and the Issues of Female Creativity," *Writing and Sexual Difference,* p. 75.
36. Thomas Hardy, *The Well-Beloved* (London: Macmillan, 1975), p. 34.
37. Although the daughter of the original Avice is not Avice at all, but Ann, Jocelyn, in his obsession, changes her name.
38. Thomas Hardy, *Tess of the D'Urbervilles* (New York: W. W. Norton & Company, 1979), p. 80.
39. Charlotte Bronte, *Life* and *Works,* VII, p. 258.
40. Charlotte Bronte, *Life* and *Works,* VIII, p. 3.
41. The title "Old Maid" can also confer power as Nina Auerbach points out in *Woman and the Demon,* Chapter IV. (Auerbach, *Woman and the Demon: The Life of a Victorian Myth* [Cambridge: Harvard U. Press, 1982], p. 109). By announcing herself as an old maid, Lily is moving outside of conventional language as she is outside of conventional marriage.
42. See Peter Gay, *The Bourgeois Experience: Victoria to Freud* (New York: Oxford U. Press, 1984), p. 5, for woman as cultural "symptom."
43. Wilkie Collins, *The Woman in White* (New York: Popular Library, Inc., 1965), p. 49.
44. For a more extended discussion of clothing, the Fall, and Pre-Raphaelite paintings, see p. 77 of this study.

Notes to Chapter V

1. Rita Mae Brown, "Feminist" in *The Hand That Cradles The Rock* (New York: New York U. Press, 1971.
2. The "male" or "phallic" "gaze" is a term out of feminist film

criticism that has paid much more attention than has literary criticism to a work's implied audience. For a discussion of feminism and audience, see E. Ann Kaplan, "Is the Gaze Male?" in *Powers of Desire: The Politics of Sexuality*, Ann Snitow, Christine Stansell, and Sharon Thompson, eds. (New York: Monthly Review Press, 1983), p. 309.

3. In a continuation of the binary oppositions that mark and delimit feminist discourse, Linda Gordon and Ellen DuBois oppose Victorian feminism to contemporary feminism in "Seeking Ecstasy on the Battlefield: Danger and Pleasure in Nineteenth Century Feminist Sexual Thought," *Feminist Studies*, Vol. 9, No. 1 (Spring 1983), p. 7. Feminism has inscribed itself in a series of such oppositions, including passive/active, pornography/erotica, and lesbian/heterosexual, that all replicate the central contradiction of male/female. Although many feminists try to dissolve these contradictions or reorient terms with respect to each other (personal/political), they still form a grid upon which feminism writes and acts.

4. Michael Foucault, *The History of Sexuality: Vol. 1* (New York: Random House, 1978), p. 3.

5. See, for example, Peter Gay's resexualization of Victorian womanhood in his discussion of Mabel Loomis Todd (*The Bourgeois Experience: Victoria to Freud*, Vol. 1 [Oxford: Oxford U. Press, 1984], pp. 71–144).

6. In this version of feminist history, the suffrage movement was the culmination of Victorian mores (see Gordon and DuBois, "Seeking Ecstasy on the Battlefield").

7. Feminists have produced such massive anthologies of women's documents as *Strong-Minded Women and Other Lost Voices from Nineteenth Century England*, Janet Murray, ed. (New York: Pantheon Books, 1982); *Victorian Women*, Erna Olafson Hellerstein, Leslie Parker Hume, and Karen M. Offen, eds. (Stanford: Stanford University Press, 1981); and *The Female Experience: An American Documentary*, Gerda Lerner, ed. (Indianapolis: Bobbs-Merrill Co., 1977).

8. The term "courtship" is particularly appropriate, both because it suggests an erotic relationship and because feminism, over the years, has been "married" to a series of other "isms," or schools of thought. See, for example, Heidi Hartmann, "The Unhappy Marriage of Marxism and Feminism: Towards a More Progressive Union," in *Women and Revolution*, Lydia Sargent, ed. (Boston: South End Press, 1980). See also Jane Gallop's comment on the glibness of such "marriages" in her introduction to *The Daugh-*

ter's *Seduction: Feminism and Psychoanalysis* (Ithaca: Cornell U. Press, 1982), pp. 1–14.

9. Robin Morgan, "On Women as a Colonized People," *Going Too Far: The Personal Chronicle of a Feminist* (New York: Vintage Books, 1978), p. 162.

10. Lucy R. Lippard, *From the Center: Feminist Essays on Women's Art* (New York: E. P. Dutton, 1976), pp. 128–29.

11. Ibid., p. 135.

12. Sandra M. Gilbert and Susan Gubar, *Madwoman in the Attic* (New Haven: Yale U. Press, 1980), pp. 93–104.

13. Nina Auerbach, *Woman and the Demon: The Life of a Victorian Myth* (Cambridge: Harvard U. Press, 1982).

14. Mary Daly, *Gyn/Ecology* (Boston: Beacon Press, 1978).

15. Elaine Showalter, public lecture at the University of Pennsylvania, April 12, 1984.

16. Monique Wittig, *The Lesbian Body* (New York: Avon Books, 1981).

17. A discussion of the literal as metaphor follows on page 193 of this study.

18. Ntozake Shange, *for colored girls who have considered suicide/ when the rainbow is enuf* (New York: Bantam Books, 1977), epigraph.

19. Leslie Ullman, "Undressing," *Natural Histories* (New Haven: Yale U. Press, 1979), p. 45.

20. I usually reserve the terms "feminist poet" or "feminist artist" for women who have explicitly declared their feminism and its importance to their work. I make two exceptions—Anne Sexton and Sylvia Plath—who wrote before the "second wave" and for whom feminist poetry could not have been a viable category. I use black women poets who have explicitly foregrounded gender issues in discussions of their work, although they might reject the label "feminist" as being a term coined and used by white women.

21. Erica Jong, "The Woman Who Loved to Cook," in *The Columbia Forum* (Fall 1972), p. 35.

22. Ntozake Shange, *sassafras* (Berkeley: Shameless Hussy Press, 1977), n. p.

23. Margaret Atwood, "Simmering," *Murder in the Dark* (Toronto: Coach House Press, 1983), p. 31.

24. Sandra M. Gilbert, "Emily's Bread," *Emily's Bread* (New York: W. W. Norton and Co., 1984), p. 35.

25. Melanie Kaye, "Jewish food: a process," in *We Speak in Code* (New York: Motheroot Publications), p. 31.

26. Kaye, "The Takeover of Eden," *We Speak in Code*, p. 63.

27. Kaye, "Amazons," *We Speak in Code*, p. 37.
28. Rachel Blau Du Plessis, "Pomegranate," in *Wells* (New York: Montemora Foundation, 1980), n. p.
29. Louise Gluck, "Pomegranate," in *The House on Marshland* (New York: The Ecco Press, 1975), p. 28.
30. Jane Creighton, "Ceres in an Open Field," in *Ceres in an Open Field* (New York: Out and Out Books, 1980), p. 57.
31. Chantal Chawaf, "Linguistic Flesh," in *New French Feminisms*, Elaine Marks and Isabelle de Courtivron, eds. (New York: Shocken Books, 1981), p. 177.
32. Adrienne Rich, "Power," in *The Dream of a Common Language* (New York: W. W. Norton, 1978), p. 3.
33. "Cartographies of Silence," in *The Dream of a Common Language*, pp. 16–20.
34. "Natural Resources," in *The Dream of a Common Language*, p. 60.
35. See the discussion of early protectionist feminism in Charlotte Tonna on p. 53 of this study.
36. Elaine Scarry, "Work and the Body in Hardy and Other Nineteenth-Century Novelists," *Representations*, 3 (Summer 1983), p. 90.
37. Judy Grahn, introduction to the "Common Woman Poems" in *The Work of a Common Woman* (New York: St. Martin's Press, 1978), p. 59.
38. Audre Lorde, "Uses of the Erotic: The Erotic as Power," in *Take Back the Night: Women on Pornography*, Laura Lederer, ed. (New York: Bantam Books, 1982), p. 298.
39. Lorde, "Recreation," in *The Black Unicorn* (New York: W. W. Norton, 1978), p. 81.
40. See Lucy Irigaray's comment that "woman has sex organs just about everywhere" in "Ce sexe qui n'en est pas un," trans. Claudia Reeder, *New French Feminisms*.
41. See Mary Daly on the revolving nature of "revolutions" in *Pure Lust: Elemental Feminist Philosophy* (Boston: Beacon Press, 1984), p. 1.
42. Daly, *Gyn/Ecology*, p. 235.
43. Jacques Lacan, *Speech and Language in Psychoanalysis*, trans. Anthony Wilden (Baltimore: The Johns Hopkins U. Press, 1982), p. 84.
44. Du Plessis, "Breasts," in *Wells*, n. p.
45. Rich, "To A Woman Dead in Her Forties," in *The Dream of a Common Language*, pp. 53–58.
46. For a discussion of women, violence, and textuality, see Monique

Wittig, *The Lesbian Body* (New York: Avon Books, 1979), p. i.

47. Olga Broumas, "Artemis," in *Beginning with O* (New Haven: Yale U. Press, 1977), p. 23.

48. Helene Cixous, "The Laugh of the Medusa," in *New French Feminisms*, p. 251.

49. Irigaray, "Ce sexe," in *New French Feminisms*, p. 103.

50. Madeleine Gagnon, *New French Feminisms*, p. 179.

51. Gayatri Chakravorty Spivak, "French Feminism in an International Frame," *Yale French Studies*, No. 62 (1981), p. 183.

52. See the discussion of Kristeva in Ann Rosalind Jones, "Writing the Body: Toward an Understanding of L'Ecritive Feminine," *Feminist Studies*, Vol. 7, No. 2 (Summer 1981), p. 249.

53. The pun is Nancy Miller's from a talk at a conference entitled "Beyond the Second Sex," at the University of Pennsylvania in April 1984.

54. For a discussion of invagination and its limitations as a metaphor for writing, see Spivak's introduction to Jacques Derrida, *Of Grammatology* (Baltimore: The Johns Hopkins U. Press, 1976), pp. lxv–lxvi.

55. In *The Teacher*, Augustine sees language, in its inability to represent fully, as a fall from truth. Written language, twice removed from its referent, is further "fallen."

56. Anne Sexton, "Menstruation at Forty" and "In Celebration of My Uterus," in *The Complete Poems* (Boston: Houghton Mifflin Co., 1981), pp. 137, 181.

57. Maxine Kumin, "How It Was," introduction to *The Complete Poems*, p. xx.

58. Rich, "Sibling Mysteries," in *The Dream of a Common Language*, pp. 47–52.

59. Lorde, "The Black Unicorn," in *The Black Unicorn*, p. 3.

60. Lorde, "Walking Our Boundaries," in *The Black Unicorn*, p. 38.

61. Daly has herself re-formed the word and its implications by splitting it up. This according to her, is *not* reform as opposed to fundamental change.

62. Judy Grahn, "The Psychoanalysis of Edward the Dyke," in *The Work of a Common Woman*, p. 26.

63. *Love Your Enemy? The Debate between Heterosexual Feminism and Political Lesbianism*, Leeds Revolutionary Feminists (London: Onlywomen Press, 1981), p. 63.

64. Jane Gallop, "Writing and Sexual Difference: The Difference Within," in *Writing and Sexual Difference* (Chicago: U. of Chicago Press, 1982), pp. 287–88.

65. Rich, " 'It is the Lesbian in Us . . .'," in *On Lies, Secrets, and*

Silence: Selected Prose 1966–1978 (New York: W. W. Norton, 1979), p. 199.

66. Daly uses the term "elemental" to conjure up female spirits in *Pure Lust*, pp. 7–11.
67. Feminists have frequently punned on the word "original" and original sin.
68. Gallop, *The Daughter's Seduction*, pp. 116, 121.
69. See Jacques Lacan, "The mirror stage as formative of the function of the I as revealed in psychoanalytic experience," *Ecrits*, trans. by Alan Sheridan (New York: Norton, 1977), pp. 1–7. For a discussion of the corps morcelé see Jane Gallop, *Reading Lacan* (Ithaca: Cornell U. Press, 1985), Chapter 2.

Bibliography

Abel, Elizabeth (ed.). *Writing and Sexual Difference.* Chicago: University of Chicago Press, 1982.

Alcott, Louisa May. *Work.* New York: Shocken Books, 1977.

Aristotle (pseud). *Aristotle's Master-Piece.* New York: Company of Flying Stationers, 1811.

Atwood, Margaret. *Murder in the Dark.* Toronto: Coach House Press, 1983.

Auerbach, Nina. "Alice and Wonderland: A Curious Child," *Victorian Studies* (September 1973).

————. *Woman and the Demon: The Life of a Victorian Myth.* Cambridge: Harvard University Press, 1982.

Austen, Jane. *Emma.* New York: Dell Publishing Co., 1959.

————. *Pride and Prejudice.* Boston: Houghton Mifflin Co., 1956.

Barkan, Leonard. *Nature's Work of Art: The Human Body as Image of the World.* New Haven: Yale University Press, 1975.

Barthes, Roland. *S/Z.* New York: Hill and Wang, 1974.

Basch, Francoise. *Relative Creatures: Victorian Women in Society and the Novel.* New York: Shocken Books, 1976.

Baym, Nina. *Woman's Fiction: A Guide to Novels by and about Women in America 1820–1870.* Ithaca: Cornell University Press, 1978.

The Bazar Book of Decorum. New York: Harper and Brothers, 1870.

Beckland, Eugene. *Physiological Mysteries and Revelations in Love.* Philadelphia, 1845.

Blanchard, Marc Eli. *Description, Sign, Self, Desire.* The Hague: Mouton, 1980.

Blessington, Lady. *The Governess.* Philadelphia: Lea and Blanchard, 1839.

Boskind-Lodahl, Marlene. "Cinderella's Stepsisters: A Feminist Perspective on Anorexia Nervosa and Bulemia," *Signs,* Vol. 1, No. 1 (Winter 1976).

168   *Bibliography*

Boston Women's Health Book Collective. *Our Bodies/Ourselves.* New York: Simon and Schuster, 1971.

Braddon, M. E. *Lady Audley's Secret.* New York: Dover Publications, Inc., 1974.

Bronte, Anne. *Agnes Grey.* Edinburgh: John Grant, 1924.

Bronte, Charlotte. *Jane Eyre.* Harmondsworth: Penguin Books, Ltd., 1978.

————. *Shirley.* Harmondsworth: Penguin Books, Ltd., 1975.

————. *Villette.* Boston: Houghton Mifflin Co., 1971.

Bronte, Emily. *Wuthering Heights.* New York: W. W. Norton, 1972.

Broumas, Olga. *Beginning with O.* New Haven: Yale University Press, 1977.

Browning, Elizabeth B. *Aurora Leigh.* London: The Women's Press, Ltd., 1978.

Bruch, Hilda. *The Golden Cage: The Enigma of Anorexia Nervosa.* Cambridge: Harvard University Press, 1978.

Cameron, Sharon. *The Corporeal Self: Allegories of the Body in Melville and Hawthorne.* Baltimore: The Johns Hopkins University Press, 1981.

Carroll, Lewis. *The Annotated Alice.* New York: New American Library, 1960.

Cecil, Meribel. *Heroines in Love, 1750–1974.* London: Michael Joseph, 1974.

Chaucer, Geoffrey. *The Canterbury Tales.* Ed. F. N. Robinson. Boston: Houghton Mifflin Co., 1957.

Chicago, Judy. *The Dinner Party: A Symbol of Our Heritage.* New York: Doubleday, 1979.

Clarke, Mary Cowden. *The Girlhood of Shakespeare's Heroines.* London: Bicker and Son, 1864, Vol. 1.

Cleland, John. *Fanny Hill: Memoirs of a Woman of Pleasure.* New York: G. P. Putnam's Sons, 1963.

Collins, Wilkie. *The Woman in White.* New York: E. P. Dutton, 1962.

Countess . . . *Good Society.* London: George Routledge and Sons, 1969.

Craik, Dinah Mulock. *A Woman's Thoughts about Women.* London, 1858.

Creighton, Jane. *Ceres in an Open Field.* New York: Out and Out Books, 1980.

Cunnington, C. Willett. *Feminine Attitudes in the Nineteenth Century.* London: William Heinemann, 1935.

Daly, Mary. *Gyn/Ecology: Towards a Metaethics of Radical Feminism.* Boston: Beacon Press. 1978.

————. *Pure Lust: Elemental Feminist Philosophy.* Boston: Beacon Press, 1984.
Defoe, Daniel. *Moll Flanders.* Harmondsworth: Penguin Books, Ltd., 1978.
Derrida, Jacques. *Of Grammatology.* Baltimore: The Johns Hopkins Press, 1976.
————. *Spurs/Nietzsche's Styles.* Trans. Barbara Harlow. Chicago: University of Chicago Press, 1979.
————. "White Mythology," *New Literary History,* Vol. 6, No. 1 (Autumn 1974).
Dewey, Mary E. *Life and Letters of Catherine Maria Sedgwick.* New York: Harper and Brothers, 1871.
Diamond, Arlyn (ed.). *The Authority of Experience.* Amherst: University of Massachusetts Press, 1977.
Dickens, Charles. *Bleak House.* Boston: Houghton Mifflin Co., 1956.
————. *David Copperfield.* New York: John W. Covell Co., 1870.
————. *Dombey and Son.* New York: New American Library, 1964.
————. *Little Dorrit.* Harmondsworth: Penguin Books, Ltd., 1967.
————. *Oliver Twist.* New York: New American Library, 1961.
————. *Our Mutual Friend.* Harmondsworth: Penguin Books, Ltd., 1978.
Douglas, Ann. *The Feminization of American Culture.* New York: Avon Books, 1977.
Dublin, Thomas. *Women at Work.* New York: Columbia University Press, 1979.
Du Plessis, Rachel Blau. *Wells.* New York: Montemora Foundation, 1980.
Edelstein, T. J. " 'They Sang the Song of the Shirt': The Visual Iconology of the Seamstress," *Victorian Studies,* Vol. 23, No. 2 (Winter 1980), pp. 183–211.
Ehrenreich, Barbara and Dierdre English. *"For Her Own Good": 150 Years of the Experts' Advice to Women.* New York: Doubleday, 1979.
Eliot, George. *Adam Bede.* New York: Washington Square Press, 1964.
————. *Daniel Deronda.* Harmondsworth: Penguin Books, Ltd., 1967.
————. *Middlemarch.* Boston: Houghton Mifflin Co., 1956.
————. *The Mill on the Floss.* New York: A. L. Burt, 1902.
Fahnestock, Jeanne. "The Heroine of Irregular Features: Physiognomy and Conventions of Heroine Description," *Victorian Studies* (Spring 1981), pp. 325–50.
Foucault, Michel. *The History of Sexuality Vol.* 1. New York: Random House, 1978.

Gallop, Jane. *The Daughter's Seduction: Feminism and Psychoanalysis.* Ithaca: Cornell University Press, 1982.

———. "Response," *Critical Inquiry,* Vol. 8, No. 3 (Spring 1982).

Gaskell, Elizabeth. *Cranford/Cousin Phillis.* Harmondsworth: Penguin Books, Ltd., 1976.

———. *Four Short Stories.* Boston: Pandora Press, 1983.

———. *Mary Barton.* Harmondsworth: Penguin Books, Ltd., 1970.

———. *North and South.* Harmondsworth: Penguin Books, Ltd., 1970.

———. *The Letters of Mr. Gaskell.* Eds., J. A. V. Chapple and A. Pollard. Cambridge: Harvard University Press, 1964.

———. *The Life of Charlotte Bronte.* Harmondsworth: Penguin Books, Ltd., 1975.

———. *Ruth.* London: Smith, Elder and Co., 1906.

———. *Wives and Daughters.* Harmondsworth: Penguin Books, Ltd., 1977.

Gay, Peter. *The Bourgeois Experience: Victoria to Freud.* New York: Oxford University Press, 1984.

Gilbert, Sandra M. and Susan Gubar. *The Madwoman in the Attic: The Woman Writer and the Nineteenth-Century Literary Imagination.* New Haven: Yale University Press, 1979.

Gilbert, Sandra M. *Emily's Bread.* New York: W. W. Norton and Co., 1984.

Gissing, George. *The Odd Women.* New York: W. W. Norton and Co., 1977.

Gluck, Louise. *The House on the Marshland.* New York: The Ecco Press, 1971.

Gordon, Linda and Ellen DuBois. "Seeking Ecstasy on the Battlefield: Danger and Pleasure in Nineteenth Century Feminist Sexual Thought," *Feminist Studies,* Vol. 9, No. 1 (Spring 1983), p. 7.

Grahn, Judy. *The Work of a Common Woman.* New York: St. Martin's Press, 1978.

Gubar, Susan. "'The Blank Page' and the Issues of Female Creativity," *Critical Inquiry,* Vol. 8, No. 2 (Winter 1982).

Hamon, Philippe. *Towards a Theory of Description.* New Haven: Yale University Press, 1981.

Hardy, Thomas. *Jude the Obscure.* New York: St. Martin's Press, Inc., 1977.

———. *Tess of the D'Urbervilles.* New York: W. W. Norton and Company, 1979.

———. *The Well-Beloved.* London: Macmillan, 1975.

Harland, Marian. *Eve's Daughters, or Common Sense for Maid, Wife, and Mother*. New York: John R. Anderson and Henry S. Allen, 1883.

Harrison, Fraser. *The Dark Angel: Aspects of Victorian Sexuality*. New York: Universal Books, 1977.

Hawthorne, Nathaniel. *The Scarlet Letter*. New York: W. W. Norton, 1978.

Heilbrun, Carolyn G. and Margaret R. Higonnet (eds.). *The Representation of Women in Fiction: Selected Papers from the English Institute, 1981*. Baltimore: The Johns Hopkins University Press, 1983.

Hellerstein, Erna Olafson, Leslie Parker Hume, and Karen M. Offen (eds.). *Victorian Women: A Documentary Account of Women's Lives in Nineteenth-Century England, France and the United States*. Stanford: Stanford University Press, 1981.

Hess, Thomas and Elizabeth C. Baker. *Art and Sexual Politics*. New York: Collier Books, 1971.

Hess, Thomas B. and Linda Nochlin (eds.). *Woman as Sex Object: Studies in Erotic Art, 1730–1970*. New York: Newsweek, 1972.

Hiley, Michael. *Victorian Working Women: Portraits from Life*. Boston: David R. Godine, 1979.

Holliday, Laurel (ed.). *The Intimate Diaries of Young Girls*. New York: Methuen Press, 1978.

Howells, William Dean. *Heroines of Fiction*. New York: Harper, 1901.

Hughes, Winifred. *The Maniac in the Cellar: Sensation Novels of the 1960's*. Princeton: Princeton University Press, 1980.

Jameson, Anna. *Communion of Labor*. London: Longmans, Brown, Green, Longmans and Roberts, 1856.

Jones, Ann Rosalind. "Writing the Body: Toward an Understanding of L'Ecriture Feminine," *Feminist Studies*, Vol. 7, No. 2 (Summer 1981).

Kaye, Melanie. *We Speak in Code: Poems and Other Writings*. Pittsburgh: Motherroot Publications, 1980.

Kuhn, Annette. *Women's Pictures: Feminism and Cinema*. Boston: Routledge and Kegan Paul, 1982.

Lacan, Jacques. *Speech and Language in Psychoanalysis*. Trans. Anthony Wilden. Baltimore: The Johns Hopkins University Press, 1982.

Leeds Revolutionary Feminists. *Love Your Enemy? The Debate Between Heterosexual Feminism and Political Lesbianism*. London: OnlyWomen Press, 1981.

Lerderer, Laura (ed.). *Take Back the Night: Women on Pornography*. New York: Bantam Books, 1982.

172   *Bibliography*

Lerner, Gerda (ed.). *The Female Experience: An American Documentary.* Indianapolis: Bobbs-Merrill Co., 1977.

Lippard, Lucy R. *From the Center: Feminist Essays on Women's Art.* New York: E. P. Dutton, 1976.

Lorde, Andre. *The Black Unicorn.* New York: W. W. Norton, 1978.

Marcus, Steven. *The Other Victorians: A Study of Sexuality and Pornography in Mid-Nineteenth-Century England.* New York: Basic Books, Inc., 1964.

Marks, Elaine and Isabelle de Courtivron (eds). *New French Feminisms: An Anthology.* New York: Schocken Books, 1981.

Mayhew, Henry. *Voices of the Poor.* Ed. Anne Humphreys. New York: Frank Cass and Co., Ltd., 1971.

Meredith, George. *Diana of the Crossways.* New York: Random House, n. d.

————. *The Egoist.* Harmondsworth: Penguin Books, Ltd., 1968.

Miller, Nancy K. *The Heroine's Text: Readings in the French and English Novel, 1727–1782.* New York: Columbia University Press, 1980.

Milton, John. *Paradise Lost.* New York: New American Library, 1968.

Morgan, Robin. *Going Too Far: The Personal Chronicle of a Feminist.* New York: Vintage Books, 1978.

Murray, Janet Horowitz. *Strong-Minded Women and Other Lost Voices from Nineteenth-Century England.* New York: Pantheon Books, 1982.

Neff, Wanda Fraiken. *Victorian Working Women.* New York: Columbia University Press, 1919.

Nightingale, Florence. *Cassandra.* Old Westbury: The Feminist Press, 1979.

Pennell, Elizabeth Robins. *The Feasts of Autolycus: The Diary of a Greedy Woman.* London: John Lane, 1896.

Rich, Adrienne. *The Dream of a Common Language.* New York: W. W. Norton, 1978.

————. *On Lies, Secrets and Silence: Selected Prose 1966–1978.* New York: W. W. Norton, 1979.

————. *A Wild Patience Has Taken Me This Far.* New York: W. W. Norton, 1981.

Rosenberg, Charles E. "The Therapeutic Revolution: Medicine, Meaning, and Social Change in Nineteenth-Century America," *Perspectives in Biology and Medicine* (Summer 1977), pp. 485–506.

Rossetti, D. G. *Poems and Translations.* London: J. M. Dent and Sons, Ltd., 1954.

Bibliography 173

Sacks, Sheldon (ed.). *On Metaphor*. Chicago: Chicago University Press, 1979.

Sargent, Lydia (ed.). *Women and Revolution*. Boston: South End Press, 1980.

Scarry, Elaine. "Work and the Body in Hardy and Other Nineteenth-Century Novelists," *Representations*, 3 (Summer 1983).

Scholes, Robert. *Semiotics and Interpretation*. New Haven: Yale University Press, 1982.

Sexton, Anne. *The Complete Poems*. Boston: Houghton Mifflin Co., 1981.

Shange, Ntozake. *For Colored Girls Who Have Considered Suicide/When the Rainbow Is Enuf*. New York: Bantam Books, 1977.

————. *Nappy Edges*. New York: St. Martin's Press, 1978.

————. *Sassafras*. Berkeley: Shameless Hussy Press, 1977.

Shelley, Mary. *Frankenstein*. New York: New American Library, 1965.

Shorter, Edward. *A History of Women's Bodies*. New York: Basic Books, 1982.

Showalter, Elaine. *A Literature of Their Own: British Women Novelists from Bronte to Lessing*. Princeton: Princeton University Press, 1977.

Smith-Rosenberg, Carroll. "The Hysterical Woman: Sex Roles in Nineteenth Century America," *Social Research*, 39 (Winter 1977), pp. 52–78.

Snitow, Ann, Christine Stansell and Sharon Thompson (eds.). *Powers of Desire: The Politics of Sexuality*. New York: Monthly Review Press, 1983.

Southworth, E. D. E. N. *Self-Raised or From the Depths*. New York: G. W. Dillingham, 1897.

Spelman, Elizabeth V. "Woman as Body: Ancient and Contemporary Views," *Feminist Studies*, Vol. 8, No. 1 (Spring 1982), pp. 109–31.

Spivak, Gayatri Chakravorty. "French Feminism in an International Frame," *Yale French Studies*, No. 62 (1981).

Stade, George. "*Parole* into *Ecriture*: A Response to Murray Krieger," *Boundary* 2, vol. 8, No. 1 (Fall 1979).

Stoker, Bram. *Dracula*. New York: New American Library, 1965.

Tate, Claudia (ed.). *Black Women Writers at Work*. New York: The Continuum Publishing Corporation, 1984.

Tonna, Charlotte. *Works*. New York: M. W. Dodd, 1847.

Trollope, Anthony. *The Claverings*. New York: Dover Publications, Inc., 1977.

————. *He Knew He Was Right*. New York: Dover Publications, Inc., 1983.

————. *The Last Chronicle of Barset*. Boston: Houghton Mifflin Co., 1974.

————. *The Small House at Allington*. New York: Dodd, Mead and Co., 1906.

————. *The Vicar of Bullhampton*. New York: Dover Publications, Inc., 1979.

————. *The Way We Live Now*. New York: Harper and Brothers, Pub., 1875.

Ullman, Leslie. *Natural Histories*. New Haven: Yale University Press, 1979.

Vicinus, Martha. *Suffer and Be Still*. Bloomington: Indiana University Press, 1972.

Walker, Mrs. A. *Female Beauty*. London: Thomas Hurst, 1837.

Ward, Mrs. H. O. *The Young Lady's Friend*. Philadelphia: Porter and Coates, 1880.

Warner, Marina. *Alone of All Her Sex: The Myth and Cult of the Virgin Mary*. New York: Alfred A. Knopf, 1976.

Wenzel, Helene Vivienne. "The Text as Body/Politics: An Appreciation of Monique Wittig's Writings in Context," *Feminist Studies*, Vol. 7, No. 2 (Summer 1981), pp. 247–63.

Wittig, Monique. *The Lesbian Body*. New York: Avon Books, 1975.

Wood-Allen, Mary, M. D. *What a Young Girl Ought to Know*. London: The Vir Publishing Co., 1905.

Index

Printed in the United Kingdom
by Lightning Source UK Ltd.
121247UK00001BA/101